No Place
Like Known
MW01624916

No Place Like Known

A JOURNEY OF SELF-DISCOVERY, CHASING DREAMS, AND FINDING HOME RIGHT WHERE YOU ARE

MEGAN VALENTINE

Published by Aradaya

ISBN Paperback: 978-1-7330429-1-8
ISBN Ebook: 978-1-7330429-2-5

First published in the United States of America by Aradaya
Printed in the United States of America

www.mvalentine.com
Instagram: @meganvalentine1

Cover Design: Aaron Campbell
Layout Design: Ashton Hauff

For the dreamers, the unsatisfied,
the ones longing for more.
It's out there. Don't stop until you find it.

Contents

Dedications And Gratitude

Dan, the love of my life and my partner in crime: it's hard to find the words to express how I feel about you and this journey we have been on. I knew you were a dreamer and a go-getter since the day I met you, but I had no idea what this crazy and amazing adventure of marriage with you would pan out to be. We've done everything from building haunted houses, traveling around the country to do hope-filled school assemblies, missions trips, youth rallies, and church planting, to living in three different states and having three kiddos—Wow, what a ride?!

I am sure I am way more than you had bargained for: fiery, passionate, and always up for a fight. I was 22 when we got married and had a lot of growing up and becoming to do. In fact, I still do. Thank you for never letting me settle along the way. For being willing to have the hard conversations because you know what I am capable of. You are truly my best friend, and I owe so much to you. I know what you are thinking, and yes, we did it together, but really. You were always ready to take the risks, and when I wasn't, you said "take my hand." You were strong when I was weak, you believed when I doubted, you were always committed to my gifts and personal fulfillment as much as you were your own. You saw greatness in me when I questioned it. You have sacrificed, prayed and advocated for my dreams, not to mention funded them, haha!

You have been at my side through the last four years of doctors' visits, surgery centers, emergency rooms, recovery, therapy, and other anxiety-inducing appointments. Though we both know you don't exactly make the best nurse, you have been so patient through my pain and picked up my slack when I just couldn't do anything more that day. You have not made me feel bad about it. You have and continue to contend for your personal health, our marriage, and our family, and for that I will forever be grateful. I am truly amazed at the life we have created with God's favor and our hard work. And what I love most is that we are just getting started! So here's to us and enjoying each day together as we make the most of this one life that we get!

Mariah, Stasia and Micah: This book is dedicated to you, my three wild and passionate dream-chasers. I love you with all my heart. You are and always have been my greatest motivation to become my best self and the reason why Dad and I have done everything we could to build the best life possible for you. You deserve nothing less than that. I hope you always know how much you're loved and valued for whom God has uniquely created each of you to be. Already you are pursuing your own dreams, and there's no place I would rather be than in the front row cheering you on. My prayer is that no matter what life throws at you or what season you find yourself in, you never lose your faith or your ability to dream. May you never settle, but always persevere and fight for what's deep in your heart. Do you! Your best you! It is my hope and prayer that the way I live my life and the message of this book inspires others to live in such a way that your world is a more beautiful place.

To Allie and A.J.: You are each one of our crew, and you know it. We love you both as our own and are so grateful that our family could fill some gaps in your lives while you filled some gaps in our hearts. You are both overcomers and stronger than you think. May you allow your pain to be purposeful, always pursue your best lives, and never let anyone or anything hold you back from getting where you want to go and becoming all you want to be.

To the Balcitis and Valentine families: I could not be more grateful for you all and being on this journey together. Your constant encouragement not just in words, but in deeds has meant the world. Whether it's praying for us, taxiing the kids, taking care of our animals, packing up your whole family and traveling to make memories with us, or just the constant support as we have moved across the country multiple times and chased some crazy dreams, we couldn't do it without you! And to all 16 of my nieces and nephews, I want you to know one of my favorite roles is being your aunt and that it brings me so much joy! I love you all so much!

To the many brave women in my family: I sit here today, so grateful to have been raised by and surrounded by so many brave women. *My mom:* who always modeled the pursuit of chasing dreams and chasing kids. *My sister:* an overcomer, a creator. and one of the best mamas I know. *My mothers-in-law:* you both have fought hard to create amazing lives and careers, and your commitment to build a blended family and put the kids before yourselves has always earned my utmost respect. *My sisters-in-law Wende and Rachel:* you are like sisters to me, and no matter what battles you are fighting, you have always been there to support me in mine. *My aunts: Loretta, Jean, Jan, Jackie:* you have gone before me ... I was young when you each dealt with deep loss, three of you the loss of spouses, two of you the loss of children, or when three of you battled cancer but your bravery, persevering spirit, and unwavering faith did not go unnoticed. I am an aunt, now, and it has been my goal to model such characteristics to my nieces and nephews, in and through all things. Thank you.

To my cousin Matt: your suicide on my 16th birthday shattered my world, but it also changed the trajectory of my life. It was in that season I awakened to the fact that we only get ONE LIFE, and it's of the utmost importance what we do with it. I will forever wonder had I reached out in your time of need if it would have made a difference. I will never know. But I did determine that I would do my best to never again miss an opportunity to bring hope, love, truth, and purpose to this hurting world, and that's the reason this book is now a reality.

To Jeanne Mayo, Jeremy and Jen DeWeerdt, Joe and Carol Saragusa, Betsy Brubaker (sorry that's who you will always be to me), Brian and Caroline Dunn, Marika Mertz, and Jackie Aillet: Thank you for seeing something in me, mentoring me, and taking a chance on me. You trusted me and gave me opportunities to use my gifts to serve the world. I will always seek to pay it forward and invest in others because of the way you invested in me.

To Beth, Paula and Erin: my leaders turned lifetime friends. I am forever grateful for your wisdom and tenacity, your willingness to pick up the phone and that you have always loved me enough to speak truth to me. You have modeled a passionate pursuit for the Lord for the last two decades and I count it an honor to be your friend.

To My Original Team Brave—Jen Jones, Thea Wood, Raquel Hunsberger, Eileen Adams, Tasha Ives, and Kelly Matlock: Thank you for being a lifeline for me in a season that I desperately needed authentic relationship, honest conversations, a safe place to go, and people to make me laugh. You all truly mean the world to me.

To the We Are Team Brave Ladies: We are almost 5,000 strong, and I know that number will multiply soon. We are imperfect, genuine, and a force to be reckoned with. As we pursue our best lives and stay committed to becoming our best selves, others will be inspired and join us. Bravery is contagious. Together we will continue to impact those around us and shape the next generation. Are you ready? I am!

Meaghan Mitchell: You were the first call I made and the first partner I had in this great endeavor. You believed in me and my vision for this community of world-changing women. You stayed patient and consistent with me as I hesitantly found my rhythm of chasing dreams and chasing kids once again. You are a true friend.

To my Optavia Family: Thank you for surprising me in all the best ways. Thank you for being greater than I could have ever imagined! The community we have in all of you is like none other. You not only make me want to be the best me and to build the best life possible for my family, but you have given me to the tools to do that. Your authenticity, love for others, and passion to make a difference allowed me to feel right at home when I was lost and doubtful.

Special mention to these Optavia greats: Eric and Raquel Hunsberger, Doug and Thea Wood, and David and Terri Miller ... you six have literally transformed our lives by pioneering the way, your consistent mentorship in our business and personal growth, and your generosity of time, energy and resources. You were just as committed to our success as we were, and our family will always be grateful. May Dan and I always serve others at the same capacity and continue to pay it forward.

Alicia Kelley: Thank you for coming alongside of me to get these words out of my heart and onto the paper. For taking years' worth of content, blogs, random chapters, notes and all the other stuff I threw at you and helping me edit this sucker a million times until the message was clear and truly depicted my heart and passion. For facing all the resistance that came in the last few months because undoubtedly this book is going to impact many. This wouldn't have happened without you.

A Note From A Mentor

Dear Friends I've Never Met,

You're holding in your hands Megan Valentine's very soul and gut. It's her personal memoir called "***No Place Like Known.***" Quite honestly, reading it may be one of the most transformational experiences you've had in years. So leave it unread at your own peril. You will be the loser. Trust me on this one.

She's given me a title that deeply humbles me: "Mentor." A pretty significant descriptive term that I'm not sure I've lived up to. But whatever my credentials, I've had the privilege of deeply knowing and loving Megan since she was an ambitious and whole-hearted young girl in high school. We've made the journey together (Megan better terms it "the battle") these past few decades. And I've been privileged to have a front row seat in her brilliant personal metamorphosis. She has a passion to partner with people to live their best lives. And from my vantage point, she is doing it powerfully.

Like many women in my era, I was made to believe that I could not chase my kids and chase my dreams at the same time. I was non-verbally taught that "good Christian women need to lay aside their own aspirations for the sake of their family." But internally, I was always restless and almost angry at that expectation. After all, the thing I most could not tolerate was being trapped in the mundane and quietly marching towards a finish line of "what-ifs" and regret.

I longed ... have I said LONGED ... for my life to be MORE. A quiet courage inside of me told me I could be my sons' "best mom in the universe" while also chasing a broader purpose with my life.

I internally knew, as Megan puts it, that "*Growth is painful. Change is painful. But nothing is as painful as staying stuck somewhere you don't belong.*" And so I can honestly say that many years later, I am perhaps one of the most fulfilled and blessed women to ever take up real estate on Planet Earth. Megan and Dan continue to play very key roles in that fulfillment.

Megan has made a very parallel journey in her life ... and is now producing fruit that is exploding off every limb of her life! This book is about that "parallel journey." It chronicles the honest, high price tags she has paid for self-discovery and finding her own personal "home." You will laugh ... you will cry. But you will NOT remain the same if you read its pages.

Her authenticity is like drinking from a surprising but rewarding well. Her humor and self-deprecation is not only just plain fun to read ... but also, deeply hope-giving. In short, this is one of "those books" that you will read and re-read because it will speak to your very core ... and challenge you to be more.

Megan references her own mantra that hangs proudly in her office. She is living up to that challenge brilliantly. But allow me to conclude by sharing an edited quote that has become a mantra for me personally. I think it echoes what Megan is calling all of us to in "***No Place Like Known.***"

> *"I will not die an UNLIVED LIFE.*
>
> *I will not live cautiously in fear of falling ... or of being pressed too hard.*
>
> *Instead, I choose to SHAKE MY VERY HEART until it becomes an impassioned PROMISE ... a soaring WING ... and a blazing TORCH.*
>
> *I refuse to live a life of undisrupted calm, placid boredom, and lukewarm mediocrity.*

Rather I, by God's grace, am determined to be an EDGE-DWELLER. I am wholeheartedly determined to LIVE OUT LOUD.

*And one day when I stand before the eternal throne of God, I will skid into Heaven and shout victoriously, '**WHAT A RIDE, JESUS! WHAT A RIDE!**'"*

So please, go get a good cup of coffee and prepare to have your life deeply impacted. This is one of "THOSE" books. The rare kind you don't encounter very often. And I am promising you this: If you allow it to, "***No Place Like Known***" will mark your life forever.

Happy Edge-Dwelling, my friend. Living OUT LOUD is a beautiful, beautiful thing.

With much sincere fondness,

Jeanne Mayo,

Megan and Dan's friend and hard-core cheerleader
Author and Public Speaker
Leadership Coach
Founder and President of "Youth Leader's Coach" and The Cadre

A Note From My Husband

Think of the most stubborn person you know. The person who won't let anything stop them. Okay, are you thinking of someone? Great! Now multiply their tenacity by 100, and you have Megan. In fact, that drive is what attracted her to me when we first met. I made her chase me for awhile before begging me to go out with her, but there was something magnetic about her unwavering faith, resolve, and GRIT that drove me CRAZY ... and still does to this day.

(Side note: She may have a slightly different version of how we met, who chased whom, and other minute details. But, since it's my foreword, you get the "truth".)

I wish everyone who picks up this book could know Megan as deeply as I do. Honestly, she's one of the greatest human beings I know. She's the kind of person who leaves tips for servers larger than the bill itself. The woman who picks up the phone to love on someone in need or coach one of our business partners, even when she's experiencing a massive migraine (because she made a commitment).

Even though we all have flaws, Megan is perfect even in her imperfections. She is exactly who you think she is. The words on the pages you are about to read aren't fake nor forced. She doesn't put on a show for anyone. She is the absolutely authentic woman, wife, mom, friend, and leader you are spending time with as you read this book.

I believe you will become a better person as a result.

You will be encouraged. You will be inspired. You will feel (and are) loved deeply. I know Megan better than anyone, so I can tell you that what you have in your hands is a piece of her, given to you for one reason: to help you chase (and catch) the best version of yourself so you can live the BEST LIFE possible. The message Megan speaks and lives out more than any other is that one. We each have ONE LIFE, and it is way too short to waste on the wrong side of fear.

I've watched Megan give herself for our children in a way that I didn't think was humanly possible. Even recently, days after a painful back surgery (and even more painful recovery), her schedule included traveling to and being fully present at BOTH Disney theme parks (yes, Disneyland AND Disneyworld, on separate coasts), for one daughter's world cheer competition in Orlando, FL and our other daughter's fine arts performance in Anaheim, CA (I will refrain from filling in the details about the emotional and physical energy involved in theme parks with kids—you get it). And in between the two, she flew with our last child to the Midwest for her mom's retirement party and a few other family birthdays. This was all in the span of THREE WEEKS!!! Oh yeah! While finishing this book.

Who does that? Megan does.

I've seen her serve our family like this, especially me, for two decades now. She has always been my biggest fan, strongest supporter, and loudest encourager. She's the only one who's never doubted even *one* of my dreams. And as a result, my life is infinitely better than it would be without her by my side.

That is what Megan does in this book—only now it's for YOU. You will get just a taste of the love and life I've experienced with her these last 17 years. Because as you read, she is about to climb into your corner and become YOUR biggest fan, strongest supporter, and loudest encourager.

Dive into these pages with your whole heart, because that's what Megan has done in writing this book.

With infinite love forever,

Danny V.

Introduction

Dear friend—

I figured I would introduce myself since I am about to bare my ever-loving soul to you. Odds are, we've never met before. My name is Megan Valentine. I am a faith-filled, coffee-loving, dream-chasing, Jeep-driving, super imperfect, totally authentic (or as my husband calls it "over-sharing") wife, mama, and coach of all sorts.

I deeply want to partner with people to live their best lives! I meet women every day and have worked with thousands over the past five years who have dreams and desires, but either they won't give themselves permission to fully pursue those dreams or they are allowing something or someone to hold them back. And I get it.

Dream-chasing isn't for the faint of heart. It's easy to grow weary when life gets hard. To want to quit when things don't seem to be working. To think you don't have what it takes because most likely you don't, at first. But I am here to tell you, to show you, that it can be done. You can chase your dreams and chase your kids. You can overcome the obstacles. You can grow into the kind of person that you need to be in order to handle your dream. It will require doing the hard work and the heart work. But—if living the life you have been desiring is on the other side, then wouldn't it be worth it?!

Four years ago, my husband and I took a leap of faith, worked our butts off, and changed everything in our lives. This book is about that journey in a nutshell, from then until now. A story where I play the role of the heroine and the villain. A story that is filled with adventure, fear, love, disappointment, chaos, gratitude, and much more. The only thing that this story does not have is regret. No regrets. Not one. Because I went for it and gave it all I had and found far more than I could have ever imagined.

Your story is being written right now. I don't know what the current chapter looks like, but I know for some reason you are holding this book in your hand ... you have been led here for a purpose. I can't promise you that this book holds all the answers to your questions or the solutions to all your problems, but I will tell you it's a story of a girl with some grit that had life-changing awakenings and experiences. And if I can do it, listen; for sure, you can do it, too.

Throughout this book, you will find quotes and scriptures that hang throughout my home or are on sticky notes in my office intentionally so I don't forget (it's too easy to get distracted and forget). Littered throughout these chapters are references to worship songs that have been on repeat in my ears for the last few years. They have kept me moving forward when I wanted to do anything but. I wanted to take you inside my story. God tells great stories. Some are in the Bible, and some are thankfully still being written with every step we take. You see, in order to chase your dreams, accomplish your goals, become your best self, and find home right where you are, you will have to ***LEAD YOUR OWN HEART***.

When the struggle gets real, the loneliness wants to consume you, the critics speak up, and the doubt starts creeping in, you will have to make a choice. Not one choice. But repeated choices day after day. Who and what will you listen to? Who has a say in where you go and what you become? Who gets to decide what you do with your one and only life? I hope it's you. The deepest, best and most authentic parts of you. Because you are the only one that has to live with your choices when it's all said and done.

I have to be honest: this book has been quite a labor of love (and I have labored three children), so what I am really saying is that I think this was even more excruciating (in all the best ways). They at least give you drugs to get you through childbirth, but giving birth to a book, especially when it's many of the vulnerable and honest parts of your own story, well that's a whole different kind of beast. I wanted to just forget it and give up multiple times. But I just couldn't. Why? Because of you, holding this book, and the chance to reach for the life you are meant to live. I believe without a shadow of a doubt that some of you will read this and you will go for it and you will get it. Whatever "it" is for you. And you need to. Your purpose is too great to stop short of anything less than fulfilling it.

> *"You were born to blaze new trails. Pioneer great adventures. Reclaim new territory. Take daring risks. You were born to tell an original story. Be God strong and foolishly courageous. Let faith not fear be your compass. Truth not lies be your guide. Always remember to give God room to prove Himself faithful. You were born for such a time as this."*
>
> – House Of Belonging

This mantra—my mantra—hangs in a large reclaimed wood frame in the center of my office. I read it aloud daily (except for the days I don't because, well ... you, know—life). But every time I speak it, I believe it even more. It resonates deep down in my soul. It waters those seeds of faith and truth in my heart. It allows me to remember that my life matters. What I choose to do with it matters. And today matters. Anyone who knows me, has heard me speak, follows me on social, or even has grabbed coffee just one time knows what I am about to say: *ONE LIFE, PEOPLE*. That's all we get. And what we do with it matters.

I may not know your name, your story, or how you got where you find yourself today. But I know someone who does. And I am quite familiar with that aching you might harbor in your heart, that longing for more. You know "it's" out there. That place beyond surface living, shallow relationships and the façade we often put forth. Maybe, like me, you've grown tired and weary of spinning your wheels while knowing that something greater must exist. Giving your best and falling short only to do the same the next day and the next. Stuck on the treadmill of life and the demands of the everyday, you feel no closer to living the life of your dreams than you did three, five, or even ten years ago. Searching for your most authentic and best self and the confidence to be her in everyday life has left you frustrated and doubting. She feels so far from your current reality, and yet your heart beats quickly at even the possibility of it coming to be. You are ready for a change.

> *"Growth is painful. Change is painful. But nothing is as painful as staying stuck somewhere you don't belong."*
>
> – Mandy Hale

Maybe we long for contentment, but sense we were created for more than just "good enough." What if there is a reason we feel that way? What if we actually were created for more? What if that longing in our souls was placed there from our Creator to call us onward and upward in our search?

I remember being at that place (more than once). Standing on the precipice of what could be a new life and looking out into the unknown. I remember being desperately scared to go for it, but also beyond excited about the possibilities that lay ahead. I think I actually began to fear not going for it and having to live with the what-ifs of regret. I didn't want to wonder what my life could have been or who I could have become. I remember saying yes, finally making a decision to go for it ... changing not only my job, but also the only career field I had ever known. Leaving my home state and packing up my family to move across the country and literally start over. On a daily basis I speak with women who are also there on the edge of change. They wake up and feel trapped in the mundane. They, simply put, long for more. Perhaps they have talents and gifts that have been forgotten, buried, they question have been lost over time. They, like me, wonder if they can chase their kids and chase their dreams simultaneously. And if so, how do you do it all? *Should* you do it all?

This book was birthed out of my personal journey (which is really just a pretty word for battle) and the countless conversations I have had (and still have) with women who struggle with this, too. You may be feeling curious or impatient to move forward and just get to what's next. In fact, I know some of you are growing weary from trusting and waiting for so long to see the desires of your heart come to life. And then there are those of you who can't imagine that what is ahead could possibly be as wonderful as what is behind you. You may feel like your best chapter is finished, but hear me when I say that God is just getting started. If you give yourself permission to explore those restless thoughts you have been avoiding, to unlock those dreams you have been holding captive, to make an intentional choice to lean in and trust God, but also to make the decision to take a leap of faith and say yes, to embrace the work found in the "messy middle" until the breakthrough happens—I can promise you not only that the absolute best is still ahead, but that you may just find it right where you are.

Would you like to join me on this journey of self-discovery, creating authentic relationships, and finding home in your pursuit of becoming fully known? You see, I began to understand as a teen that I was known and accepted by God. I learned along the way that life would be more full if I allowed myself to be known by others. But what I didn't realize until recently was the power of knowing myself. I have come to find that ...

> *When I am operating as my highest and best self, authentically and confidently me, doing actions that are congruent with my personal beliefs, and pursuing the seemingly terrifying dreams that reside deep in my heart, I am more fulfilled.*

And when I am fulfilled, I am my best me. That is when my family, friends, and all others around me receive the love they deserve. If that's what you desire ... to become the best you and to live your best life, then you picked up the right book and you showed up to the right place.

Call it a quest.

... a voyage.

... a journey.

It doesn't matter. What matters is that we are willing to open our hearts, minds, and spirits to what God wants to speak to us specifically and to the possibility that going all in could revolutionize our worlds as we know them.

Will it be easy? Nope.

But will it be worth it? Absolutely.

So if you are ready, let's go! And if you are at all like me, you will realize that this will be so much better if you have people alongside you. Would you consider inviting a few of your people along on this journey with you? Maybe even order a couple of them a book and agree to meet up for coffee once a week. Or if life is too crazy, just start a text group. In the meantime, do not let fear, doubt or discouragement get the best of you. Don't believe that just because you *bought* the book, you have taken the step. Walk in to what "could be." Don't slow down or settle for where you are when you know He has more.

Don't close the book when you simply need to turn the page.

Your next adventure is being written as you sit here today. The answers to your questions are just around the bend. The twists and turns will reveal their purpose. God will work all things together for your good.

Seriously, He is shaping and crafting you, preparing you right now for the next stage of your destiny. That scary but exciting stirring you feel within? Don't ignore it. Go with it. You don't have to trust me yet, anyway. Just keep reading.

CHAPTER ONE

The Stirring

"We have two strategies for coping:
The way of avoidance or the way of attention."

– MARILYN FERGUSON

I awoke to another busy day at the Valentine home, pretty much our norm at this point in time. My husband was a full-time executive pastor at a large church, and I was the high school youth pastor. Days were fun—but super long. Most nights were full and weekends, too. My time was often consumed with activities, meetings, counseling people, prepping messages and services, retreats, conferences and camps. Honestly, though, I absolutely loved ministry life! I thrive around people and really enjoyed the incredible team I worked with and was in awe at some of the amazing things we were accomplishing.

I felt God's path for me was full-time ministry (at the early age of nineteen!) and had chased after it with passion. But now our girls were six and four years old, and we had a new baby boy, Micah. By this time, we had already ventured across the country and back again on ministry adventures that we loved, every one different from the other. But I began to feel torn, pulled in so many directions that it was becoming difficult to switch hats. There was what I wanted to do, what I felt God had for me, and the daily tasks of what needed to be done in my role as a pastor. Then, of course, I was feeling the need to be more and do more to meet the needs of my children. I struggled consistently with the fact that I felt like I could never win at motherhood and ministry at the same time (oh and I think marriage was in there somewhere–sorry Dan ☺). Yet I felt so strongly that I was supposed to do it *all*.

How many of us have felt—still feel—that way?

So I did what I knew to do and sought counsel from other mothers in ministry, I made constant adjustments, and did the best I could in both worlds.

Though good things were happening, I would never claim that I was killing it.

I don't remember the time of day or the chaos that was most likely ensuing as I began my normal routine of emptying the girls' backpacks and lunch bags like always. I took out their folders and began to look at their papers, their notes from the teachers, and their little pictures and crafts from that day. I picked up a little project that Stasia (four years old at the time) must have worked on with her teacher. There were two columns with Stasia's little pictures next to an adult's handwriting ... one was titled "What Stasia likes," and underneath were the words "unicorns, rainbows, and candy." No surprises, there.

The other column was titled "What Stasia doesn't like" and underneath were the words "Sharks, the dark, and hurrying up."

I laughed out loud. How funny is that?

But inside I knew.

I knew the moment that I saw that. If I'm being honest, I knew it before then. That little piece of paper confirmed the internal cringe I had been feeling.

Something needed to change. How many times was I trying to hurry this little slow poke along because I was under-organized and overcommitted? We were constantly on the go with places to be, people to meet, things to do and we were almost always running late. I knew our family couldn't thrive if it stayed this way. But I didn't know what to change, how to change it, or even where to begin.

Two of my children, for the most part, just rolled with our very full calendar, the multiple events and different babysitters, the guests in our home, the on-call nights and weekends.

But one of our kids didn't. Guess which one?

Stasia, our middle child and a complete creative from the get-go, was not thriving in the life we had created, or maybe just allowed. She needed more quiet, more routine, more sleep, more one-on-one quality time. I don't know if you have one of these kiddos, but she needed more from me than I felt capable to give. I am sure the other two, though not as outwardly evident, needed more, too. And if I were to be brutally honest, as selfish as it sounds and as difficult as it is to confess, the whole thing didn't feel fair. Here I was trying to serve God and be a good steward of this life, these talents and this calling, and now these three beautiful children. Why did I have the desire to do it all and feel like I was supposed do it all, if I couldn't do it all well? And what was I supposed to do about it? Honestly, I didn't know how to fix the cycle, and it just became an acceptable way of life.

I became aware pretty early on that to be the parent my kids needed, (especially my little, creative Stasia), I would have to change and become a better me. At times, I didn't feel best suited to be her mother. I battled with dark thoughts, like that she deserved more than someone like me. I looked around at other moms who confidently felt they were supposed to stay at home and have their family be their sole focus, but I didn't feel that. Was *I* supposed to feel that way? Then came the guilt.

I saw women who were more patient and more consistent, kind and soft-spoken, who threw Pinterest-level parties and cooked gourmet-type dinners every night (or ordered them from somewhere that I have not discovered yet). I admit I often thought about how my kids would probably be way better off with one of those moms. But God gave these little beings to me because he knew we needed each other. Stasia, too. Not because she and I are the same, but for the exact reason that we *aren't*. What if to be what she needed, what all my kiddos needed, would require me to change—not just myself, but also life as we knew it? Was I capable? Was I willing to do it? What would that even look like? Wait—what about those other ambitious dreams in my heart?

I thought about what I wanted for me and what I wanted for her. What did I want the *most*? And I thought about that little preschool project. It is now eight years later, and I *still* think about that project, those words and that little girl who was not created to operate at such a crazy pace. I had an awakening from that preschool picture: *this* grownup girl (the creative's mom), wasn't created to operate at that pace, either.

A year or two later, I had the privilege of hosting one of the main guest speakers for a women's conference our church held every year. This conference increasingly began to draw sought-after speakers from across the country, and honestly, I could not have been more pumped! The speaker I was to host was someone I have looked up to for many years. I actually was chosen to be her host because it was well known that I personally admired this woman and aspired to be like her. I had traveled to see her speak multiple times, read many of her books, and done her Bible studies on my own and in groups (talk about SuperFan). She was not simply someone I wanted to meet; she was someone I wanted to be (now I just sound creepy, but roll with me here). I mean, how awesome would it be to get to travel and speak to women around the world, to bring the Word to life and to awaken others to what is possible?! I didn't want to be her ... but well ... I wanted to be *me*, living a life *like* her. And I believe my motives were pure. It was not because I wanted money or notoriety; it was because I really wanted my life and my gifts to inspire people to become more of who God wanted them to become—to reach as many people as I could with the story of hope and possibility. Since God had dramatically changed my life, I was all about dreaming big and not living small.

Because of all those things, when the day came, I headed to the airport super early (I had to make that first impression a good one!). I pulled up to baggage claim in arrivals, which I had firm instructions to do, versus parking and walking in. I was greeted by those oh-so-kind people in the neon jackets who began waving and yelling at me to get moving, so I circled as I waited for a text from the speaker's assistant. And I circled the entire airport, coming around to baggage claim again. And circled. And I circled again.

It was 45 minutes before I received a text that they had landed and now were waiting for bags. Okay, fine. I was just excited and ready to be the best host ever ... and so I kept circling. Five more minutes ... ten more ... fifteen ... now the texts were coming in from the conference staff, concerned about our guest getting there on time. The speaker had the preference of booking her own tickets and had chosen to arrive *right* before she needed to be there. I was starting to feel a little stressed, knowing we would be driving back in classic Chicago rush hour traffic, but remaining positive. I said to myself, *it's all good; I got this!*

The text I had been waiting for finally came through, so I pulled up to the door. Before I could even get out, the speaker and her assistant both hopped in the back. As I started to introduce myself, the speaker said, "If it's okay, we are just going to both ride back here because we have some things we need to talk through and take care of."

"No worries!"

Hmmmm ... So that didn't go exactly how I thought it would. That's all right. I have got a couple of days with her to make a connection.

I focused on driving as she ran down a list with the assistant on what she needed for her next trip, talked about booking a few other speaking engagements and other calendar items and deadlines, and then jumped on the phone for the remainder of the 80-minute drive. We made it to her first engagement with time to spare ... Pretty sure it was about two minutes to spare, but hey, we made it.

It all seemed a little chaotic to me, but her message was amazing! And all went well (except when she became publicly frustrated with the media team for not getting her slides right—but shhh—actually, those guys, who I know hadn't slept for days to make sure every detail was done right, had the slides in the order they were sent with the instructions—or lack thereof, as sometimes happens—that they were sent, but let's keep that to ourselves ☺).

Later that night, I brought the speaker and her assistant to their hotel and checked them in. I said, "Here is your schedule for tomorrow. Would you like to go over it so that we can ensure that you have everything that you need?"

"Nope; we are good and have everything we need, thank you. See you tomorrow."

(Looking back I should not have asked but just started going over it … Hindsight is annoying. Or 20/20).

So, here's the CliffsNotes version of the ending. The next day, she got her schedule mixed up and didn't realize she was speaking when she was supposed to and made that apparent, not to her hosts, but to the audience! From the stage, she apologized while looking directly at me and said she had been given "miscommunication." (Can I be honest? I may have shed a few tears during that session out of sheer embarrassment and feeling like I did not live up to my job and had let others down who trusted me, though I knew I had tried).

When the session was over, she walked off the stage. It was a bit awkward … we headed to her last speaking engagement for the conference when we met up with her assistant, who—even though it was her first time traveling with her—received quite an earful about how it was all *her* fault.

We walked to the session and were talking through her flight time when I realized that the time we were told she would be leaving and her actual flight were different. She was scheduled to speak from 12-1, but I learned that she had a 3:15 flight. The airport is at least 80 min away with traffic. She told me she was fine getting to the airport an hour before and that she did it all the time.

Who would be in trouble if she missed her flight?

We rushed in, started her last session, ended it early, and practically ran to the car and sped to the airport.

By this point I was feeling pretty drained, but I did my best not to get stressed and finish this job strong. (I probably forgot to mention that I don't think I have the spiritual gift of hospitality, specifically when it comes to hosting guest speakers and to please never ask me ever again?) I realized that on this particular weekend. This time, she sat up front with me and proceeded to tell me to "hurry" and "just speed" and "just go around that car"... "Come on, you can go faster!"

I promise I am not joking. Though I didn't pause to look at myself in the mirror, I could feel that my face was flushed, my heart rate was escalated, my palms were sweaty and for the love of God, could we just get there?

I have never been more relieved to drop someone off at the airport and I legitimately prayed for her assistant's well-being the whole ride home.

But for real ...

But. For. Real.

I remember thinking, "What the heck just happened?"

What a whirlwind. I found myself on the ride back to the conference unsure of what I felt, or even why. I was disappointed. I was angry. I was honestly confused. I thought to myself ... Well, now I know ... I'll read her book ... But I don't want to be her friend and I definitely don't want a life like hers.

Wow ... That's harsh ... And honestly how I felt after my up close and personal encounter. (Now to balance, I know many others have had countless amazing experiences with her, so I know it's not like that all the time).

Driving back, I was admittedly frustrated, not only with the situation, but also with my ugly thoughts and what now seemed like ridiculous and apparently unrealistic expectations. Thankfully, I had some time to work through it. I said, "God—I know that you allowed me to experience that for a reason, but can You help me understand? Help me understand how someone can desire to impact a large crowd but make no effort to connect with individuals? How can someone be effective where they are right now if they are caught up in where they are headed next? How can someone who loves people so much not notice the way they treat and talk to others, especially those right next to them?"

And then a humbling moment in the car ... A full calendar, endless commitments, pressing deadlines, a fast pace, trying to be everything to everyone. Don't get me wrong—I know the things she is doing are all good things, and dare I even say all God things? But at what cost? And I don't even know her. Here's the thing, though ... I know *me*. And I know what those things can do to me. Let me rephrase: what those things *were* doing to me.

And I didn't share all of this so that you would be disappointed in her, or feel bad for me, or think that all those amazing women who are writing books and speaking from stages at conferences aren't who we think they are, because in reality they aren't. They're just like us. (I'm writing this book and prepared to most likely disappoint some of you before you even finish it.)

I felt that day that the Lord whispered to me, "I allowed you to see and experience this because it is sometimes how people feel when they are on the other side of you. This is the path you are headed on, and if you get more on your plate, without figuring things out, this, too, will be *your* future." Hmmmm ... Silence. I didn't have much to say, but a lot to ponder.

It was a quiet drive back to what was left of the conference, a quiet that I would later realize was a necessary element of my stirring.

Two more years later, we were approaching our oldest daughter's tenth birthday. I couldn't put my finger on it, but for some reason this event was really messing with me. My first baby, the one that made me a mama for the first time, was turning ten. Mariah was entering the double digits and getting closer to becoming a teen. I had the stark realization that if she were to leave for college at 18, then she actually had less time left with us in our home than she had with us up to this point.

WHAT THE CRAP?!?!

Sorry. I know that's a little crass, but I see all you ladies in your "I love Jesus, but I cuss a little" shirts, and I figured I would be okay.

That's exactly where I was.

This thought haunted me daily, and I couldn't shake it (Hint: The Stirring). Why was I feeling this way? Probably most mothers do, right? At certain ages, we just get emotional and miss the baby we once had. We become aware of how fast time is going. And it was all of that, but more. The realization that I have only one life to live and one season with my children in my home was hitting me so much more deeply. I pictured myself ten years from now (when she would be 20) looking back. What would I be thankful for? What would I regret? What could I never get back again?

I decided to do something a little different from what I normally do and actually gave myself permission to be brave and take the time and space to dig a little deeper into this strong emotion percolating inside of me. I found myself starting a conversation first with myself, and then with my husband.

"Honey, our daughter is turning 10. A decade has flown by. What do we REALLY want the next decade to look like?! Do we want these next 10 years to look like the last 10 years? Because if not, the time to change **IS NOW**."

The truth is, I have worked with teens and families for a long time. And I have seen it happen over and over again and again. We get stuck in a rut in life. We allow the days, the weeks, months—and before you know it—the years pass by. Or maybe things are good, nice and comfortable, so we just keep doing what we are doing as if it's, well, you know ... "just what we do." We don't hit the pause button often enough to stop and to consider, to evaluate and to dream, and to pray to see if maybe, just maybe, there might be something different, something new or quite possibly something even greater out there for us. We feel a stirring for something more, but we ignore it. We sense something or someone trying to get our attention, but we breeze right past it. Sometimes things even stop us in our tracks, but we just won't go there. We pray and talk to God, but we don't take time to listen to Him, and we avoid quiet, let alone meditative solitude, at all costs. We simply don't give ourselves permission to explore and dig deep.

WE FEEL A STIRRING FOR SOMETHING MORE, BUT WE IGNORE IT.

Stop.

Breathe.

Listen.

What we know is if we even travel that path mentally, let alone in real life, it could mean change. It could be scary. It would mess with our comfort level. It would require risk, and most certainly, it would not be easy.

Let's be real for a second ... who wants to purposefully dive into ALL that?! (I mean come on ... I am so tired as it is that I don't even want to wake up 20 minutes earlier to shower. Instead I make the hard decision of hat day or dry shampoo.)

Not to mention ... what would other people think? How would it affect the people around me? What if I fail? And even if we paused long enough to answer half of the questions I just asked, most of us have already opted out by now and fled back into the routine of life as we know it.

How dare I say such things, you ask? Because as you can see, I myself have avoided the whisper, turned away from the idea of change and shut down the process long before it even began. So the voice within grows quieter, and more time continues to pass by.

Our one and only life continues to pass by.

I felt it that day in the kitchen as I held that art project in my hands. I sensed it after the conference as I was driving home. And many times in between. I knew Mariah turning ten was bringing me to a crossroads that was calling for a decision. So I took some time to think about the last ten years, not just through my eyes this time, but instead through hers. What aspects of our family life were not just working but were truly thriving? And what aspects were not? If I had a clean slate, a fresh white canvas, what kind of life would I design for my children? What would that look like, feel like? What did I want, versus what did they need, in this next season?

WHAT DID I WANT, VERSUS WHAT DID THEY NEED, IN THIS NEXT SEASON?

This was not an easy process, but I knew it was the start to an amazing adventure. My husband and I had pioneered adventures before, though, so I knew how tough they could be and how much time it could really take before things actually made sense and fell into place.

Yuck.

Did I really want to shake things up again?!

Looking back, I almost have to laugh about the fact that I had absolutely no clue how different this adventure would be from the others we had taken. But I think God knows it's best we not have the details, as we often wouldn't embark into the unknown if we knew what we might have to journey through. We simply have to trust that if He is stirring us, and if we are obedient to go where He is calling, it will be worth it.

And here is where we choose which "what if" we focus on. I had to move through the what-ifs of possible failure, regret, disappointment, and insecurity to get back to that place where the "what if" of possibility resides. What if we really do serve a God who knows the longings of our hearts because He put them there? What if He really does want more for me and for my family than even I want for us? What if what He promises in His Word is true?

Ephesians 3:20 in the Message version says, "*God can do anything you know—far more than you could ever imagine or guess or request in your wildest dreams! He does it not by pushing us around but by working within us, his Spirit deeply and gently within us.*"

I love this. I needed this. This is what I felt taking place: A deep and gentle work happening within. I didn't feel pushed, prodded, or forced. I felt the warmth of His presence reminding me that He created me and loved me and that I could trust him with my fears, my dreams, my future, my children. If this—God doing far more than I could ever imagine or guess or request in my wildest dreams—is what is waiting for us on the other side of trust and obedience? Then I'm in. At least—I think I'm in.

Wouldn't it be worth it? I have come to find when talking to most people that their regrets center not around the things they *have* done, but the things they *haven't* done, the things they feared to "go for."

I couldn't ignore The Stirring any longer. I didn't know what was ahead, but I knew it was time to say yes to God once again and to take the leap, even if it meant I wasn't sure where I would land.

CHAPTER TWO

Blank Canvas

"When there is nothing, there is
the possibility of everything."

– ANN BRASHARES

Once I finally allowed myself to slow down enough, to be quiet enough, to recognize that little voice, that whisper, that *stirring*, I began to lean into that feeling and start to imagine what could be *different*.

Initially, nothing happened because Dan was not ready to even go there, and my thoughts were too immature to do much with them. Many of us respond this way, because the stirring also leads to the unknown, maybe even a risk. This can be exciting, but also terrifying. I mean, we simply don't know what to do with those stirring thoughts. Is this just a *wish*? Is there something I'm supposed to be *doing*?

I know many adults who experience the stirring—maybe God is bringing back a dream that has been buried in our hearts for so long, or something He put deep within many years ago. It can be exciting to remember what you used to want, or to realize that something new might be on the horizon. Allow yourself to figure out why you're feeling that way, why this keeps coming back up, why your pulse races when you think about it, and maybe why you don't even want to pray about it.

The problem is, most people stop right there. They feel the stirring, but don't do anything about it. We tell young kids, "Dream big! You can do anything you want to!" We ask high schoolers, "What do you want to do with your life?"

But then as adults, we get stuck believing that whatever we chose to "do" at 22 or 30 is what we inevitably chose for our lives. Forever.

"Most people don't lead their lives, they accept their lives."

– John Maxwell

Studies show that making a decision to do something "I'm going to make ______ change" releases the same dopamine in the brain as actually making that change. Therefore, many people never make the actual change. The act of dreaming is exhilarating, but without the partnership of action, dreaming alone does not move us forward.

It just doesn't have to be this way.

We need to give ourselves permission through each and every season to determine what's right for right *now*. It may not be the same thing as last season! If we are unsettled or restless, those feelings are worth exploring. If you could actually stop, give yourself an afternoon to be introspective, dream, imagine. What things would surface?

I continued to lean into that stirring I was feeling as the days passed, and one day, I decided to just sit down with my journal and really think about what could be next if I got to design my future ... a "blank canvas," if you will. I began to imagine what life could be like if no responsibilities held me back. If I didn't feel tied to my title. If I didn't worry about what people would think. And I began to write down the way I wanted my life—my best life—to look. It was exhilarating, exciting, and again, scary. Was it even possible? Fear was still trying to creep in. I hadn't yet gone all the way in actually believing that things could change.

"Sometimes we have to let go of the life we have planned, to have the life that is waiting for us." – Joseph Campbell

After much prayer and doing my best to listen, weighing things out and doing the blank canvas exercise, seeking wise counsel and lots of conversations with my husband, I said yes to one of the stirrings in my ear, and I laid my dreams on God's altar. In October of that year, I resigned from my job as a youth pastor, a job I loved and couldn't believe I got to do, following my mentor in her exact role. I told our senior pastor (my boss) that I didn't know what was ahead, but that I did feel this was to be my last year as the youth pastor, and that if possible, I would love to stay through summer camp and prepare a team for my transition. I wanted the opportunity to finish strong and well and was grateful that he gave it to me.

I would like to tell you that I was confident I had made the right decision and assuredly knew that God had great things ahead, but honestly this was a move more out of obedience and for my family's best than it was for me personally—or at least that's what I allowed myself to believe at that point.

Lest you think more of me than you ought, allow me to confess that in the same meeting that I resigned, I also cleverly attempted to pitch a different job for myself. Not only that, but this potential job didn't exist yet. I presented a great plan, or so I thought, of launching a moms' ministry and running it part-time as a branch of our women's ministry. [*Sigh*] How do you couple walking in obedience with downright fear and self-reliance? Just like that.

But this was only one piece of the puzzle in our lives, and once I made this decision and began to move forward, it was like a cloud lifted. Even though I had no details, I sensed a serious peace that God was working.

You see, in this season, I became more aware that things were already starting to shift. Dan had made a deliberate choice to get healthy a few months back and was doing amazingly well, so I decided to jump on board in order for us to take the journey together. He was now down almost 50 pounds and more energetic and excited about life than I had seen in a long time! He was no longer just surviving each day, but he was ready to thrive and dream again. My prayers were being answered right in front of my eyes.

I was so proud of his journey that I posted on social media about his weight loss and how great he was doing—Whoa! I was not prepared for what happened next. The response was downright shocking. Hundreds of people over the next few months reached out to us, wanting us to assist them to get healthy and live their best lives.

I couldn't help but keep pondering the blank canvas exercise and the dreams we had written down. What was God up to?

Were we ready for this? Life was already crazy, yet we couldn't help but assist these people. We discovered through their courageous vulnerability that so many people that we loved and had known for years felt stuck and hopeless—and we actually had a tangible solution. These friends were not living out their optimal lives by any stretch; many were pastors and leaders around the nation who were confident in front of the crowds, but off of their platforms, were insecure, frustrated, and lacking self-control. Assisting them to be their very best in all areas of life would have a ripple effect, and now that we knew that, we couldn't deny this door that God had opened. So we began to offer health and hope simply by sharing our journey and living it with confidence.

One of those loved people we were excited to share with was Dan's dad. He had been unhealthy for quite some time, and the fact that he was ready and willing to pursue health was amazing! Unfortunately, within a week of reaching out and making that decision, my father-in-law was diagnosed with stage 4 lung cancer.

Obviously, this was devastating. Christmas was around the corner, so we decided to head to Phoenix to be with Dan's family and make as many memories as we could with the time that we had left.

Our trip ended up being wonderful. As we were packing up on our last day, Dan looked at me and said, "What if we move our flight back a day or two? I'm not ready to go back."

I laughed. But then I realized he was serious. I reminded him that we didn't have money for flight changes for five people, but then suddenly realized something more was going on. I had recently been learning and practicing the skill of digging deeper and really listening (thanks to my mentor, Raquel), so instead of assuming or jumping to conclusions like I normally would, I said, "Honey, let's talk about this. Why don't you want to go back?"

He talked about how being in the sunshine and the fresh air made him feel joyful and alive. He loved Phoenix and talked of needing a break from the routine and the pace, the weather, the pressure he was feeling (mostly self-induced). I could tell he had been holding so much in, not wanting to rock the boat or mess with our security.

Let's be honest: this wasn't ideal. And he knew it. Here I had just recently resigned. We had purchased a beautiful home and were still just getting settled. We were living near my family and raising our kids with the most amazing church support system, and they loved their friends and school. I mean, yeah—I told God blank canvas—but this was taking it to a whole new level.

You see, I've watched people feel the stirring; some even get to the blank canvas exercise, but many stop there. There are no limitations as children, no boxes to fit into. In order to move past the exercise and put wheels on it, we have to slow down, release fears, and almost recapture that childlike aspect of dreaming about something and believing it can happen.

We as adults have now experienced disappointment, unmet expectations, and criticism, so we automatically think, "I'd love to do that, BUT ... what if I can't make it work? What if I can't find a different job? What if people think I'm crazy?"

It gets to the point where we stop even saying, "I'd love to do that."

We think we're being realistic.

In the Christian world, sometimes those fears can come under the guise of, "I don't know if that's God's will for me." We stop there, waiting for a sign in the sky.

But let me ask you this: if you have a desire in your heart—if you are loving God and serving God and reading His word and spending time with Him—and you have a dream in your heart, why would you *not* believe that this dream is from your Creator?

If it is something that is way bigger than you and something that would benefit others around you, force you to become a better version of yourself, and bring glory to God ...

Why would you *not* believe that He put it there?

And ...

Why would you *not* go for it? Trust me, if He doesn't want you to do it, you'll know along the way.

Maybe a better what-if would be, what if it *does* work out?

It's going to take a fight, but God wants to grow you into who He wants you to be by fighting for this dream He's put into your heart.

When Dan began to talk to me about staying in Arizona, I was already in a season of surrender and stirring, praying and seeking (otherwise it probably would have sent me into a sheer panic!). I had literally posted on social this quote the day before our conversation:

"Change happens when the pain of staying the same is worse than the pain of change."

– Tony Robbins

My caption below it read:

When what you desire becomes larger than the price you have to pay to get it—how badly do you want it? What are you willing to change to get it?

As I described earlier, Dan and I were living a life that can only be described as chaotic—calendar always full, his things, my things, youth things, church things, school things, sports things, passing kids off to each other, or babysitters ... you know how it can be. One aspect we wouldn't cross the line with, though, was date night. We considered that a priority no matter how crazy life got; however, we were usually too exhausted to do anything much more creative than dinner and a movie. It didn't matter, though, because it was time together and time away from the kids, and we needed it.

After Dan lost almost 80 pounds and rediscovered his energy, confidence and zest for life, date nights started coming alive again. The conversations started shifting from how was work and anything new with the kids—to future dreams and possibilities. Can I just say how much more fun that was?

Coming back from Phoenix, we went on to have lots of blank canvas conversations, and they weren't just about what *he* wanted or what *I* wanted or what *we* wanted for our kids, but it was also about the two of us, and our family as a whole. We coined a phrase that was actually birthed out of those date nights: "napkin dreaming." Still to this day, we share about our tradition of napkin dreaming and how much it has positively impacted our lives and our marriage.

I'm sure you know how hard it can be to have an actual adult conversation when there are multiple kiddos running around, vying for your attention and interrupting you every three minutes. So each week, by the time we got to date night, we had so much to talk about. We quickly realized that those times together were vital to our relationship as a couple.

One night, we were passionately talking about all the things we wanted to do and all the places we wanted to go ... dreaming, planning, wondering what the future held. Dan looked across the table said to me, "We need to write this stuff down." I, of course, hadn't brought a notebook to date night! So he grabbed the only thing that might work like a piece of paper. A napkin.

Through those next few months we started intentionally going into date night with a blank canvas mentality. And we filled tons of napkins. Napkins that we still have today because they were imperative on our journey. And many of the things handwritten on those napkins have come true.

We asked ourselves if we could design and create a life for our family—a blank canvas—what would it include?

- A life where all three of our children could thrive, but also ...
- Dan and I could use our talents and passions to impact and serve others
- Time and financial freedom
- Sunshine and outdoor living
- Memory-making experiences and travel as a family
- Ability to bless our family, loved ones and church
- Friends who are like family so we can enjoy life together
- The means to give generously whenever we felt led

We had to figure out: what were our personal values? What were our family values? If we wanted to be remembered for certain things, what were those things? How do we begin to implement these things into our family?

AM I GOING TO SAY YES TO THE LIFE THAT I DESIRE? THE LIFE I KNOW MY FAMILY NEEDS?

Am I going to say yes to the life that I desire? The life I know my family needs?

Saying Yes

What often happens when you begin to blank canvas your life is that you can get to the point where you're able to imagine the possibilities. The struggle then becomes—how do I get there?

I'm looking at my canvas; my dreams that are bigger than I am. They seem crazy. I look at it and have butterflies in my stomach, partially because I'm excited, partially because I'm anxious. And THEN—I get paralyzed. I come to a crossroads and have to make a choice:

1. *I am going to do this! But I don't know where to start.* OR ...
2. *I can't do this. It could cost me too much.*

For me, the biggest key was looking back at all the other times I had said yes. How did those turn out? Not bad at all. In fact, my best life flowed from those times.

I get brave when I think of my sixteen-year-old self, walking away from all my friends and my boyfriend to follow God. To go to a retreat where I'd be challenged to give God my whole life for 30 days—just 30 days, and I did.

Did it work out?

Yes! I began the best adventure of my life.

I get confident when I think of saying yes to a ministry internship instead of college, even though it was not what my parents wanted and was against all their plans. It set the course and trajectory for my life the past two decades.

Was it worth it?

A thousand yeses!

My faith grows when I think about the experience of breaking off a wedding engagement and trusting my broken heart and deep-seeded dreams to the Lord. How that difficult and bold decision led me to the love of my life, Dan Valentine.

When I look back on the mile markers in my life, I was afraid to head into most of them. But what if I hadn't said yes to some of those choices? What if I wouldn't have taken that 30-day challenge? What if I would have just gotten married when I knew it wasn't right?

Ask yourself what I did: Do I want the next ten years of my life to look like the last ten? If not, what am I going to do about it? Because if I don't do *some*thing right now, everything is going to stay the same. Will I regret it if the next ten years is a repeat of the last? And remember, it's not just about you. What does your spouse need? Your family? There is a way to create a life that is what you all need and desire, so don't grow weary fighting for it.

It doesn't matter how old you are, how tired you are, or how far you have traveled in one direction ... it is never too late to pursue your dreams and live the life you were meant to live. If you are longing for more, it's for a reason ... you were meant for more. Stop the pity party, wish your doubt farewell, toss your excuses in the garbage disposal and hit the button. Today is your day. The time is now. Make a decision to go for it. Whatever it is for you. You only get one life.

"There are far, far better things ahead than any we leave behind." – C.S. Lewis

God had been preparing my heart. From our five-year stint of living in Florida, I knew that both Dan and I thrived more in the sunshine and in year-round outdoor living conditions than where we had to fight the winter "blahs" and try to choose joy so many months of the year. We both loved Phoenix and had talked of moving there when the kids were gone or when we retired, but to leave everything and life as our kids knew it right then?

Moving away from my family would hands down be the hardest part by far, but I knew in this season that it was my responsibility to make sure my five would thrive. Our little tribe. To do what was best for my husband, our marriage, our kiddos and to have no regrets with this short time the five of us would be together in one house.

The next few weeks, Dan and I continued to talk and pray, and by the end of January, he resigned. We planned to transition after summer camp, the same time my tenure would end. Our plan was to pack up and leave northern Illinois and move to Phoenix, Arizona, in order to be near Dan's dad for his last few months.

Honestly, we had such a peace about Phoenix, but where we would live and work and those kinds of details—you know, the semi-important ones—we weren't quite sure about. Not as much peace, there. As the move grew closer, I kept coming back over and over again to the story of Abraham.

God told Abram: "*Leave your country, your family, and your father's home for a land that I will show you.*" Genesis 12:1

This was going to be a move of obedience before details. What a huge lesson! You want to talk about faith? Stepping out and into what you know God is telling you to do before you even know *how* He is going to do it is some hard stuff! Yet, so often, God leads us one step at a time and is faithful to provide along the way if we do our part and trust Him to do His.

So we were praying, hoping, believing, and acting as if He would show up and fill in the details. We focused on finishing the last chapter at the church strong and well, and we continued to assist others to get healthy and become their best selves and loved being able to do so. We kept praying that *God, would you please reveal more about what the next chapter is going to look like*?

We had a few church connections in Arizona and sought conversations with them because that's what we do and have always done ... work at a church. Why would it be any different this time? Well, living a life of surrender, daring to say yes and dreaming with a blank canvas sometimes leads you to do things you have never done before. As we continued to pray and look at all of our options, we did not have a peace about working at any of those churches. We felt strongly that this health coaching we were doing truly was the ministry where God was calling us. We were watching people's confidence be restored, marriages that before were struggling now thriving, and parents who now had energy to engage with their children at a new level. People who were holding back had a newfound freedom and lease on life.

I watched my husband and how much he loved it. It was such a natural fit for him. He was made for ministry and business, and this allowed him to do both. He absolutely loved one-on-one coaching, giving people practical tools and seeing people's lives change. We were growing our own team of coaches, and he excelled at training teams and leading leaders.

But me? This was a bit of a new world for me. I wasn't sure if I was ready for new. At least *this* much new ... new state, city, school, church, career, schedule, friends ... right? New EVERYTHING. I felt like I was leaving behind my sweet spot and all I had ever known. But I refused to be the one to hold him back when literally this was everything I had been praying for Dan. So I said confidently, "Let's do it!" while my real thoughts were consumed by questions like, *what is this going to look like? What will people think? Is there a place for me as well as my gifts in this next season?* I honestly had more questions than answers, but there was no stopping us now.

So mid-July we loaded up everything we own ... well honestly we loaded up half of what we own because the truck wasn't big enough to hold it all! We did a quick purge, which was pretty representative of this next season, and I hopped in the driver's seat of the minivan for the 30+ hour drive with three kids, a cat, a rabbit and a guinea pig. Ready or not new life!

Here we come.

CHAPTER THREE

New

"Forget the former things; do not dwell on the past.
For I am about to do something new.
See, I have already begun! Do you not see it?
I will make a pathway into the wilderness.
I will create rivers in the dry wasteland."

ISAIAH 43:19

The raw truth is that sometimes ... new sucks. Sometimes it feels like a "dry wasteland" longer than a fresh beginning.

That's kind of what I experienced. I needed one of those rivers.

Let me explain.

We made it to Arizona. The first couple weeks felt like we were on vacation ... umm—except the living out of boxes part. Then it quickly became time for the kids to get ready for the new school year. I was excited, but also more than a little nervous (scared?). Change is hard, even for people who are pioneers and like to try new things (and especially for the pioneers' children who really had no choice in the matter). The unknown is always lurking ...

When we got to our new city, I started figuring out the things that you figure out.

- Will we work at a church again? If so, which one?
- What would be my new, go-to grocery store? How would I find a new physician? New dentist? New orthodontist?
- How do I help my kids make new friends?
- How do I make new friends?
- How long will it take me to get back to my new house without the help of my iPhone?
- Where can I plug in and make new commitments to connect and serve?
- How much do I do in this new season?

That's a lot of *new*.

To add more intimidation, we were now self-employed exclusively for the first time ever. That meant there was no welcome wagon waiting for us, no announcement at church on Sunday that we were the new staff members, no one waiting to greet us at our house—it was a very different experience than those past moves. And we had to figure all this stuff out ourselves.

When you're suddenly alone and everything is different, it's easy to slip into a dark place. I wanted to protect my tribe of five.

I will never forget the first day of school in this new place. I reiterated to my kids that "we can do hard things." Encouraging them all the way to the school, I dropped them off, and then shed a few tears and prayed that someone—anyone—would be nice on this first day. And maybe someone might be nice to me, too?

I remember thinking about them and murmuring quiet prayers all day. Although we had made the decision to move for the good of our entire family, I knew that change and new—these things are hard. Really hard. Combining them is even more difficult.

Let's just say that day one wasn't a good day. And I could barely get them up and out the door the next morning.

Isn't it true that when you're in the new place, nothing feels like home?

I so wanted it to feel like home for them.

But by the end of day two, my oldest was telling me how she met her new best friends. Things were looking up!

But my sweet, then-third-grade middle child, Stasia, informed me that, "these aren't my people." Her new teacher had mispronounced her name that day. To my sensitive Stasia, if you can't pronounce her name correctly—well, you don't *know* her. She didn't even want to talk about it. She just wanted to FaceTime Papa (my dad), which made her feel better for the length of the call. Then we cried together because we both missed Papa, Grammy, and everyone else.

I didn't know how to fix this "new" thing, but I knew as their mom, I needed to. If I'm being honest, it felt a little bit like ... scratch that ... let's go with ... a lot like I was failing. I hadn't made friends here. Stasia wasn't making friends, here. How could I lead her when I wasn't getting it done for myself?

She was missing "home" in Rockford. And I was, too. I needed to find a way to fix this.

First, I decided that with all my new free time, I needed to start volunteering for every open spot at the school and whatever church we chose—and anything else I could do. To avoid feeling the pain and fear of "new" and—yes, failure—old habits resurfaced. I made myself as busy as possible so that I simply would not have time to feel those feelings.

I also got very determined to help her make friends. I will never forget the time when I worked up the courage to approach another mom to ask if her daughter would like to have a playdate with Stasia sometime. Her response? "Oh, we don't do playdates. We just don't have time for it."

As I said, when you're suddenly alone and everything is different, it's easy to slip into a dark place. So I just started filling up that calendar, like so many times before. Old habits die hard.

It got to the point where my schedule was full, but my soul was empty. All those things I used to blame for my overly full calendar—ministry, church schedule, kids' activities—truly, none of this existed in this new period. Yet here I was, making my schedule overly full once again, with nothing to blame this time except myself.

IT GOT TO THE POINT WHERE MY SCHEDULE WAS FULL, BUT MY SOUL WAS EMPTY.

I didn't have anywhere I *had* to be. I didn't *have* to book as many meetings or appointments, but I did. If I kept myself busy, I didn't have as much time to think about the hard stuff, right? All that chaos and noise would block it out. And let's just get real for a second. I never personally felt like I was meant to be a stay-at-home mom, and now here I was, working from home while my kids were in school, granted our youngest only part-time.

I couldn't help but start to recognize that for all these years it was my default to blame ministry, my position, or others for the fact that I couldn't always be present, prioritize my children, or have a meal on the table. The God-honest truth is that being a mom is so hard—for me, anyway. These little people require so much time and energy, and so many decisions and so much responsibility comes with raising them. Motherhood is the hardest and greatest challenge (and privilege) I have ever been given. And I felt inadequate for the task every day.

Not to mention I could spend all day cleaning, and you couldn't even tell (not that I did, but if I had—well, you know what I mean). I could grocery shop, meal prep and cook an "amazing" dinner that half the family wouldn't even like, the rest would be done with in three minutes, and then the kitchen would be a mess all over again (let's not even talk about the laundry situation). It was an ongoing cycle that never left me feeling appreciated or noticed, or like what I was doing with all my time even mattered, because that's Mom Life. All these years, I had excuses and reasons why I "couldn't" do those things. I would instead go into a job where I could work hard, invest energy and time, and see measurable results. I was consistently given affirmation and encouragement and that drove me to grow, build, and succeed which lead to more confidence and fulfillment.

I didn't feel like I was succeeding at motherhood, especially in this new season. Why did it seem to come so naturally for other women and feel so hard for me? I guess I just thought it would be easier once I was in charge of my time. Boy, was I wrong. Making the decision to move to what felt like paradise: outdoor living, sun shining, a beautiful home with a pool, working together with my husband and getting to do it from home and on our terms? How could it get better than that?! My previous expectation had been, "*Sure, it will be an adjustment as far as outside relationships go, but it will be fine! This will bring us all so much closer and give me the availability to be the kind of mom my kids need.*" Makes sense, right?!

Ummm … yeah. It was not that simple. It didn't take long for me to realize it wasn't the outside factors that were the problem. Rather, it was me all along. But with everyone else getting adjusted and how unsettled everything still was, I just couldn't go there emotionally. So I stuck with what I did best, and I stayed busy. It was easier than slowing down enough to really think about how much my kiddo was hurting or how unfulfilled I was feeling. I knew time would help—I just wasn't sure how to speed up the process or where to even begin.

Unpacking

I remember a few months after moving, my husband looked over at me one morning, pointed to a pile of boxes in the upstairs hallway and said, "Hey, honey—I think it's time to finish unpacking."

Once we had gotten to Arizona, I was highly motivated and determined to get everything unpacked and settled. I started with the kids' rooms, then our room, and eventually moved on to all the main public areas that other people would walk through or see. Let's do this!

But then—you know how it goes. Life happened. Things got crazy, and I got comfortable.

I pretty much stopped noticing the boxes that were sitting in the closets and piled up in the corners. It had become my new normal, and I just quit seeing them. (That box in the back corner belongs there, right?)

When Dan told me "you gotta unpack those," I walked over and I peeked into those boxes, my boxes, and immediately was overloaded with anxiety. I knew that I would have to sort through that stuff and figure out where it was all supposed to go, and if it even had a place here in this new house and this new chapter of our lives. Did I just need to let some of that stuff go? Doing the work of sifting through not only the actual items in each box, but also all the memories attached to everything in there—well, it completely overwhelmed me. It wasn't just *stuff*—it was our life in these boxes. Our past. Old habits and lifestyles. Items that represented good seasons and some not so good.

Let's be honest. Sometimes it's hard to sort through all that stuff because it's not stuff. It's emotions, memories, dreams too.

Admittedly, every area in our home that might be seen by outsiders appeared clean and in order. I had actually set up just enough to be good enough. If I had to dig everything out and sort through the contents of all these boxes, it would be quite a messy process. One I would rather skip, if at all possible. But since I'd tried that (and it obviously wasn't flying with the hubby), I hesitantly peeled back the cardboard folds of the first box and discovered sermon notes, cards from students, and memories from the two different youth groups I had led over the last eleven years.

Okay.

Now it was clear to me why I hadn't gotten to these boxes yet. I was avoiding dealing with the emotions that would come with going through them. As I sat on the floor organizing all these precious memories into piles, I felt God whisper to my heart, "This isn't really about unpacking the boxes. This is about areas in your mind, heart, and life that you need to unpack. Areas that you need to sort through, and some of them don't have a place here where you want to go and in who you want to be in this new chapter."

THIS ISN'T REALLY ABOUT UNPACKING THE BOXES. THIS IS ABOUT AREAS IN YOUR MIND, HEART AND LIFE THAT YOU NEED TO UNPACK.

I knew He was right—the same way that my husband was right about unpacking, but that didn't make it any easier to start. I had a choice to make. Would I keep asking my family to just co-exist with the big brown boxes? I mean, I watched the next morning as my girls had to go out of their way and turn sideways to get around the boxes just to go from their bedrooms to the bathroom. They did this unconsciously because this was the routine since moving in. They were just used to it being that way. Really?! That's ridiculous. My kids should be free to walk and run around without these obstacles. What kind of mom does that?!

This Mom.

This Villain.

Guilty.

I started to wonder what other things or parts of me was I asking my family to coexist with? Things that would probably appear obvious and ridiculous to a houseguest, but they were so habitual that I didn't even see them. Why is it that I put so much effort into looking good on the outside to the people who in 10–20 years most likely won't even matter to me, yet the guard is down with my family, my tribe, the ones I love most?

I STARTED TO WONDER WHAT OTHER THINGS OR PARTS OF ME WAS I ASKING MY FAMILY TO COEXIST WITH?

Living as a fast-paced, driven woman for so long, I had allowed unhealthy habits to develop that were becoming more and more apparent in this *new* season (you know, the season I had blank-canvased for?). I was kind to acquaintances, uplifting to friends, yet short with my husband and kids. I chose to be ON for clients and co-workers operating with grace and positivity and would turn OFF after my meetings or phone calls and nag, complain, and be frustrated with my family. Not intentionally by any means, but let's be honest: intentions don't matter; reality does.

I was often too tired to play, too busy to really listen, and absolutely done by bedtime. The fast pace had fallen away; the full calendar and deadlines set by someone else were no more. Yet, there I was: still me. I could no longer blame fast-paced ministry, anyone or anything else for my habits and attitudes. It was time to cut the crap, get real, and ask myself some difficult questions.

Was I going to continue to force my family to co-exist with me and my undeniable issues (and the boxes)?

I knew my kids should never have to tiptoe around me or be afraid to upset or annoy me. They should be free to run around and be kids who are growing and thriving. I long for my kids to look at me and see who they want to become—versus the opposite. You know what I am talking about, right? You hear grown adults talk about how their parents or home life affected them, and it seems to go one of two ways. I am who I am or I do what I do either *because* of my mom/dad or *in spite* of them. I so badly want to be a because of and not an in spite of. But I was starting to awaken to the truth that it was going to take some work.

I desire a husband who falls more in love with me every day instead of one who avoids me because I am always being negative about something. I don't want to be an obstacle to those whom I love the most. I don't want to hold them back. I want to be the gateway through which they discover joy, purpose and love. I want to be the one modeling freedom, faith, and passion. I want to link arms with them as we all pursue our best lives, my voice loudly cheering them on in all seasons.

I DON'T WANT TO BE AN OBSTACLE TO THOSE WHOM I LOVE THE MOST.

Galatians 5:22–23 (TPT) describes the woman I desire to be and reminds me that it can't happen purely because I decide it, or muster it up, or grit my teeth and force it:

"But the fruit produced by the Holy Spirit within you is divine love in all its varied expressions:
joy that overflows,
peace that subdues,
patience that endures,
kindness in action,
a life full of virtue,
faith that prevails,
gentleness of heart, and
strength of spirit.
Never set the law above these qualities, for they are meant to be limitless."

Those are qualities I would like to be known for. How I want those closest to describe me. But here I was on the other side of making all these changes on the outside in order to design a life where I could focus more on family and be more intentional with the time I have left with my kids at home. Yet, as I started to take a long, hard look in the mirror, I realized none of that would matter if I didn't commit to transforming what was on the inside. Sure—things were good enough on the surface and to those who looked on from a social media standpoint or someone who dropped by for a visit, but this was not enough. I was meant for more. I was meant to be more. I needed to unpack those boxes.

So there I was. I finally realized that upon moving to Arizona, I had become desperate for purpose and fulfillment. I had been trying to fill the voids and easily spent my time and energy, but pretty much felt like I was running in circles and getting nowhere. The days passed, and I found or created things to do—but they weren't *my* things. They were other people's things. I wasn't doing things that lined up with my unique God-given purpose, or so I had convinced myself.

Now don't get me wrong. I would wake up every day and open the blinds, walk onto the patio, and literally say out loud, "thank You, God, that I get to live here." The sunshine was revitalizing to me; I felt like I could breathe for the first time in a long time. I knew that this move was what we all needed. And yet I just floundered in trying to find my place in this new life.

Through business and busyness, I was avoiding. And procrastinating. And hiding. Here I was trying to create an identity for myself, as well as a life where I could matter and be seen out of fear that God was done with me. Out of insecurity that there was no place for me. Out of the lie that my "glory days" were behind me and certainly not ahead of me.

Not really intentionally or consciously. But who has time to be intentional and conscious when you are just running on the hamster wheel of life? Kids, school, building our business, investing in people, volunteering, homework, dinner, bedtime. Wake up and repeat. Then you find yourself running on empty. Again—I knew there had to be more. And a better way. But what was it?

There were days I loved this new way of life. And there were days I felt lost and alone. On one of those days, my husband turned to me and asked what was wrong. I told him I was having a sad day. Let's just say I don't remember the exact conversation but it went something along the lines of—isn't this what you wanted, and why are you not done with the sad days yet? I mean it had been months and I should be over it by now. HA! I love my husband and he honestly meant well. He hates seeing me sad and desperately wanted to fix it. But I just had to explain that we were different—you know, that whole men-are-from-Mars-women-are-from-Venus thing? And that I was literally mourning the loss of a way of life that I knew and loved for the past two decades, not to mention all the people that went with it. And that it didn't mean I wasn't thankful for what we have now.

Emily P. Freeman shared something in her book *Simply Tuesday* that resonates completely with where I found myself so frequently that first year: "My friend and author Leeana Tankersley says often we fear if we admit we're struggling, it may mean we're not grateful. But the truth is, we can be struggling and grateful at the same time. I think I recognize in myself a hesitancy to admit my struggle for fear it will incriminate me, branding me as a woman who has a beautiful life but doesn't appreciate it."

WE CAN BE STRUGGLING AND GRATEFUL AT THE SAME TIME.

I did have a beautiful life. And I did appreciate it. But on some days I still needed to grieve the loss of what was.

Grief comes in waves.

Sometimes there would be sad days, and that was okay. I knew if I didn't give myself permission to be sad or at least identify those feelings that I would implode, and nobody needed that, I tell ya! The Pixar kids' movie *Inside Out* had just been released before we moved. Perfect timing, seriously! It totally hit home with me as both my daughter and I were going through similar emotions as the main character. I easily wanted to push Sadness away and try to let Joy run the show. But I had come to learn that without sadness, there can't be joy. The depth of sadness often reveals the depth of love. When I am grieving over the loss of someone or something, it means that I had the opportunity and gift of deeply loving them.

When I am able to view it this way, I can honor the sadness and even find joy in it. I don't have to be imprisoned by it. Nor do I have to pretend it's not there.

Unfortunately, I have experienced much loss and been to way too many funerals in my lifetime. There are normally two types of services: the kind that is sad and disheartening, focusing on all that was lost, or the alternative: a celebration of the life that was.

I decided it was time to throw a funeral for my old life and chose to make it a celebration. So I did break out those boxes and sort through them and cry as I read the notes and remembered what those items, tokens, and pictures represented. Not sad because they are no more, just grateful that they ever were.

I knew it would be a hard, messy process to do the inner work of digging and sorting, both in the boxes and in me.

But it was long overdue. Without a shadow of a doubt—in order to be who God created me to be in this new season and be the kind of wife and mom and leader I longed to be, I had to unpack and release a lot of mindsets and habits that I had picked up along the way. I had work to do.

> *"Maybe the journey isn't so much about becoming anything. Maybe it's about un-becoming everything that isn't really you so that you can be who you were meant to be in the first place."*
>
> – Paulo Coelho

Easier said than done for sure. I am still a work in progress. Even as I write this I can think of times this week where I fell back into being that woman from the past. But she is not me. And I will keep fighting to be me, the real me, the best me, full-time.

Maybe today you find yourself in a place of doubt, wondering if you can *really* do it. Can you push through? Can you keep going? Will you ever overcome?

You may be starting to question if you have what it takes to get through this season. Breakthrough feels so far away. Please let me tell you that it's not. Success is not only measured when you can check the box, say you did it, and celebrate the win. Success is also finding the magic right there in the middle. It is searching for the treasure in the mundane and ordinary. The win is being honest with where you are at, making the most of today and yet choosing to not stay there. It's leaning in to the growth that needs to take place in you so that you not only get to the other side, but become who you need to be in order to handle all the things you don't know about that are up ahead for you.

So ... trust the process. Be intentionally conscious today to be grateful for where you are. Keep your eyes and your heart wide open ... don't miss what God desires to reveal to you because you may feel like you are in the thick of it. The good news is, "new" doesn't last forever. Pretty soon, things will start to feel like home.

CHAPTER FOUR

Build Your Team Brave

"Find your tribe. You know the ones that make you feel the most YOU. The ones that lift you up and help you remember who you really are."

– JENNIFER PASTILOFF

I remember the time I had the honor of playing the important and pretty vital role of "field trip mom" for our middle child, then ten-year-old Stasia, who I may have mentioned once or twice, already ☺. She was elated to miss school in order to head to "Main Event," a venue that offers bowling, laser tag, a huge arcade and ropes course all in one. So we pulled up that morning and the kids followed us in, piling off the bus, galloping through the parking lot, and bounding through the front doors of the building. Our senses were immediately overloaded with bright lights, flashing signs, loud music, the sound of games, and the smell of pepperoni pizza. No matter which way we turned, it seemed a million things were happening.

The teacher gathered the students, divided them into groups, and assigned them each a chaperone. My crew of girls ran off to play a couple of games, and then their eyes caught sight of the sky course—yep! A ropes course set up high above the arcade. They were enthralled and giggling with excitement, so we headed over to the entrance and realized the time slots were full for a couple of hours. No worries! We had a great time bowling, playing games and laser tag while we waited.

Finally, our much-anticipated time slot approached. We got in line, handed the bored worker our tickets, we began to get suited up in our harnesses. The girls were getting giddy and then a little wide-eyed as our harnesses were tightened across our backs, waists, and thighs, and we got anchored into our rope and into the metal system that ran across the top of the course. Everyone was breathing a little more quickly, and I heard more than one squeal. I loved experiencing the joy of all of these girls!

We started up the staircase—these girls were ready! This is what they had waited for all morning! We climbed to the top where there was a clear view of the beams, bridges, and ropes, AND a clear view of just how high up we really were, far above everyone below us. The girls crossed over the first section, which was pretty secure, and then came to the middle where they had to pick a direction in which to go. The choices were a bridge with big gaps between the steps, a skinny beam, or a thin rope. We were at a crossroads, if you will.

I looked over at my daughter and I saw fear and panic sweep over her face. She was so excited all day that I didn't think for one second she would get scared. But she did.

She had been ready; she held great anticipation for how this experience would go, yet then we finally arrived, and it was totally different from what she expected.

Fear set in.

Looking down at the heights, the realization of how high up we were, the ground ahead not looking secure—it was all too much.

I could tell she wanted to get down, to be done. But she had come too far. She literally couldn't turn back now. There were people behind her, and she had to keep moving forward. I went first so that I could be on the platform, waiting for her. I called out to her, but she was frozen, wide-eyed, staring at me and shaking her head.

What could I do?

I leaned towards her and confidently affirmed, "Stasia, lock eyes with me, look at me; you are anchored in. You can trust the anchor, you can trust the system, you are not going to fall ... You are anchored in; you are safe. Look at me, look down, take a step and look back at me. You can do this."

I began to coach her through her fear. I stayed "happy," smiling and excited, telling her, "This is fun! You are doing great! You are so brave. You got this! One step at a time." Thankfully, I realized that she needed that assistance to move forward through her fear so that she wouldn't be stuck or paralyzed. I wanted to help her experience what she had hoped and set out to do.

What I have come to find as I travel through life is that people have dreams in their hearts, lives they want to experience, and things they long to do.

I do. I bet you do, too.

Sometimes we set out to do these things and are really excited. We anticipate greatness, success, victory, and fulfillment, and *then* we start the journey. Often before we know it, we get to this place where we look around—and fear sets in, just like it did with Stasia. Fear takes over, we aren't quite where we thought we would be, and things look different than we had planned. We are facing these obstacles and challenges, and we need to be reminded of the same two things that Stasia did that day.

The first is that we are anchored in. We are safe. If we are anchored into God and into His Word, we can take steps of faith. We don't have to rely on ourselves, on our own abilities or strengths, because we are anchored to Him and relying on him.

Today I want to encourage you to take your eyes off of your circumstances, off of your fears, yourself, and to be able to put your eyes on Him and remember what He has promised us.

Hear what the Lord is saying in Isaiah 41:10 (MSG) and picture Him speaking directly to you today:

"Don't panic. I'm with you.
There's no need to fear for I'm your God.
I'll give you strength. I'll help you.
I'll hold you steady, keep a firm grip on you."

No, really. Close your eyes, take a deep breath, and envision him speaking this peace giving truth right to you. Read it out loud. Write it down and hang it up. It's so easy to forget His incredible promise. To doubt his presence in the midst of whatever we may be facing.

If He calls you out into the unknown, the uncomfortable or the unexpected, you can trust Him. You are not alone. He is with you! Even if the ground ahead seems shaky, you can have faith that you are secure. If you are anything like me, you would prefer if He let you in on the plan, the timing and oh, you know—every single other little detail. He may only reveal one step at a time, but that may be all we need (or all we can handle).

I know this stuff is easier said than done. It's easy for me to tell you all these things confidently because I know it's true. I have lived it and seen it, and yet in the middle of it I had to tell myself this again and again. And I am sure that in the next situation I face, I will have to do the same. I remember the months leading up to our big move, I would have a peace that what we were doing was right and yet, still totally doubt myself. Some days I would be so excited—other days I would be scared to death.

I would listen to "Oceans" by Hillsong United again and again to build my faith that I could do it. I felt like Peter stepping out of the boat—I wanted to trust, to keep my eyes fixed on God. I so badly didn't want fear to distract, paralyze, or rule me. So I would listen to those lyrics on repeat to intentionally feed the faith inside of me and starve the fear.

The second truth we need to remember is that once we know we are anchored to God and secure in Him, we need some people on the other side. We need people who are willing to lean in and lock eyes with us when we get stuck, when we are paralyzed. They are people who know us, who know the purpose and dreams deep in our hearts, who see our potential and are unwilling to sit by and let us settle for anything less than what we are capable of.

> *"Surround yourself with the dreamers and the doers, the believers and the thinkers, but most of all, surround yourself with those who see the greatness within you, even when you don't see it yourself."*
>
> – Edmund Lee

Get some people who believe in your dream and believe in you. These are the kind of people who won't let you quit when you get scared, and they won't let you give in to discouragement when things are different than you thought they would be. Nope! They call you onward, speak life into you, aren't afraid to challenge you, to make you better and to stand by your side through it all.

"SURROUND YOURSELF WITH THE DREAMERS AND THE DOERS, THE BELIEVERS AND THE THINKERS, BUT MOST OF ALL, SURROUND YOURSELF WITH THOSE WHO SEE THE GREATNESS WITHIN YOU, EVEN WHEN YOU DON'T SEE IT YOURSELF." – EDMUND LEE

The Bible talks about these kinds of people in Proverbs 27:17: "As iron sharpens iron, so one man (or woman) sharpens another."

There is mutual benefit in this kind of friendship ... each being made better by the other, each becoming more efficient for their God-given calling and purpose.

I remember that when I first gave my life to the Lord at sixteen, I had to shift my friendship circle. You see, I had learned from previous experience that I could not keep hanging out with the same old people in the same old places and expect to be different. That had failed me in the past, for sure. So I had to want all that God had for me badly enough that I was willing to change the main influential voices in my life. This meant altering key relationships and friendships. It also equated to getting to a place where His one voice of approval drowned out all the other voices of disapproval. I had to follow that whisper in my heart and do what I felt was right for me, even if it cost my popularity and acceptance. To take the path that may have been less traveled but offered me congruency, peace, and fulfillment. Isn't this still what we long for? It looks different in every season, but this congruency, peace, and fulfillment ... this is home.

This is always home.

Our youth pastor Jeanne Mayo would always tell us, "show me your friends and I'll show you your future." Sometimes (probably too often), we would mock these statements as they were repeated again and again. I tell you what, though ... we didn't forget them. And some of us even went on to be youth pastors who repeated the same statements to their youth groups (and were mocked, too).

Mockery or not, even back then I knew it was true for my life. And I knew I needed to find some people who had faith, boldness, and a passion for the Lord, or mine would soon fade. I had not found my voice or personal confidence yet. I knew I was a follower who desired to lead but wasn't strong enough yet. I needed some people headed in my desired direction to go before me.

Being intentional to have the right people up close to me has been one of the best decisions I ever made and have continued to make for the last couple decades, for sure. I remember when I went up to one of the "Christian" girls at my school a little mortified and I said to her ... "Hey, so ... I made a decision at retreat to really live for God, so I am going to need some new friends. You think maybe you would be willing to call me and we could hang out this weekend? I am kind of afraid if you don't, I might go back to my old friends and the parties, but I really don't want to" (No pressure!).

Looking back, I am kind of amazed at my bravery. But I will tell you—there is power in hope. I had hope that God had that more I was looking for. So if it meant asking for help, reaching out and feeling ridiculous but finding some friends, then I guess I was willing to do it. Not I guess. I mean, I *did* do it. And I made two friends. Two girls very different from me, but two girls who cared more about what God thought than what others thought. Two girls who were passionate in their personal pursuit of God and lived their faith boldly. Two girls who didn't judge me based upon my past, but they saw my hope for a new life and met me where I was and took a risk on me.

HOW BADLY DO YOU WANT TO BECOME THE BEST VERSION OF YOU? ENOUGH TO ASSESS THE KEY RELATIONSHIPS IN YOUR LIFE?

How badly do you want to become the best version of you? Enough to assess the key relationships in your life?

I learned all of this again when we left Illinois the first time to work on staff with a church plant in Florida.

Those first few months, loneliness set in. All my friends were far away and busy. I was struggling to find people who wanted to make the effort long distance, and I really didn't want to be the needy friend. I would catch myself taking it personally when no one would call or answer my calls and wondered if it were just time to move on.

In this season, I learned to—once again—pray for the right people to come into my life. Something cool happens when you start consistently praying for something ... you also open your eyes and start looking for the answer to those prayers. So I started looking for friends, but not just anyone. I looked for key people who shared similar beliefs, women who would add value to my life and liked to have fun. I was looking for women who were passionate about loving God, living an abundant life and being true to themselves. I was a new mom. I needed some amazing mamas in my life. I was a new youth pastor. I needed women who understood motherhood and ministry and the chaos of it all. With such a new and very busy season in my marriage I needed friends who prioritized their marriages and had relationships I admired.

There were ladies everywhere around our community, our church, my kids' preschool, gymnastics program, etc ... so how did I find the women I could personally connect to? I had to start showing up, start being fully present, asking questions, listening, and offering invitations. Play dates, coffee dates, etc ...

I have found that the majority of women *do* desire authentic relationships, those that delve below surface level conversation, friendships that make them better—but not all women do. And even the ones who do? Many don't know how to even begin, how to go there. There is just something in us as women ... we battle feeling like we are either not enough or quite possibly too much. So we hold back and try to put forth what we think others want to see and hear, what we feel is acceptable. But life is too short. I want more than that in my friendships.

When making the decision to move to Arizona, I knew this time—because of our experience of moving to Florida—I knew how hard new seasons could be. And this time would be like none other. Not only were we moving to a new city, state, and part of the country—we were in essence changing career paths. It felt like we were changing literally EVERYTHING. Maybe not. But it would look and feel different. I knew it was the right decision, but I also knew it would be hard, a kind of hard that I had never experienced before.

What could I do to be ready?

Deep friendships would be vital in this season of my life; I knew it. I am so grateful that just before we left Illinois, I attended a powerful women's conference at our old church. There, my friend Jen DeWeerdt shared about the journey that her conference staff had taken throughout that year. Through a series of events and meetings as they planned and prepared, they began to orchestrate more than a conference. There in that circle of ladies, they openly shared their setbacks and fears, and they encouraged and empowered one another to move forward and chase dreams. They all set some pretty big and brave goals and committed to keep each other accountable. They started calling themselves "team brave." A group of them decided to go sky-diving, one moved forward with the dream of adoption, and one set out to write a book. Jen challenged us that weekend to go create our own team brave.

I knew right then and there that was what I needed. I had lots of friends and fellow pastors that I did life with currently. But I had been there before. When you leave, everything changes for you, but the hamster wheel of life, careers, and parenting doesn't stop for them. People are busy, but maintaining healthy, strong relationships is imperative. I had to figure it out.

I realized pretty quickly that in order to find what I was looking for in this next season, I would need to create it. I would need to be the kind of friend I wanted.

Live boldly, "do you," and you will attract others with similar interests, common core values, and like-mindedness. I guess this can be good or bad.

"Your vibe attracts your tribe."

If you don't like whom you are attracting, it's time to take a good, long look in the mirror. You really do attract who and what you are. I have had to learn how important it is to "be more interested than interesting"—how to quit trying to get everyone to like me and set out to celebrate and honor the greatness in them. Talk less and ask more questions. Genuinely listen and remember what they say. Actually pray for them and care about what they care about.

I consider myself so many people's biggest cheerleader. I absolutely love seeing people win at life, relationships, accomplishing goals, really, everything! It is my favorite thing to genuinely celebrate with them and for them. This one consistent choice, along with intentionally being a positive voice and a bright light amidst a lot of darkness and negativity, has helped me find my people, and it just may help you find yours.

Phoenix would be the first move where we showed up to our new home and no one would meet us on the other side of the moving truck to help us unpack and get settled. There wouldn't be anyone to greet us who was willing to show us around or help us maneuver all the newness. We weren't going to be brought into a ready-made community of people on Sunday morning as the new pastors, so if I wanted community, I was going to have to build it from the ground up.

I simply had to be intentional in the area of friendships, especially in the season of in between. I thrive with people, working on a team, in a circle. I process best in conversations with others, and I was about to be working from home with my husband in a new career field. Let's be honest: he loves me, but he does not want to sit and talk with me for hours of the day as I process, create, and bring things to life. And there's nothing wrong with that. But I just knew I would need more and that it would require me to step out beyond comfort zone to get it. It would have been easier not to, but I learned a long time ago a catch phrase that has kept me going along the narrow road: "It's not easy, but it's worth it."

So I decided to just go for it.

"If you really want to do something, you'll find a way. If you don't, you'll find an excuse." – Jim Rohn

I made what felt like a terrifying decision. I decided to try to start my own team brave. I needed something that could ground me and get me through that season. I needed women who had the capacity to make a commitment. I needed women with whom I felt I resonated when we talked. I needed women I could trust and who would be willing to take the friendship circle to the next level.

I reached out to six women I knew would inspire and help me and just asked them all to meet me at Starbucks to share something with them. All six women actually showed up, and some of them didn't even know each other, yet (they do, now!). I thanked them for coming and introduced them. At this point, the women knew we were making this big change and moving to Phoenix. I made myself very vulnerable and said to them:

"This is what I know. I'm about to change every part of my life—in every way. And I know that if I don't have a circle around me that will support but also be honest with me, this will be an even more difficult and lonely journey. I am looking for women who are willing to be authentic and vulnerable. Girls I can laugh with and cry with. People that actually pray for and prioritize each other. Women who don't compete with, but rather celebrate with one another. Each of you are amazing, and I know you have so much to offer the other women in this group. So I guess my question is: Do you want to be a part of this circle? And not only offer those things to me, but to each other and me to you. Essentially, I need some friends. Will you be my friends?"

I gave them all journals and team brave shirts and told them not to answer that day. It was bigger than a quick decision; it would take commitment to stay connected as we all lived in different areas of the country.

May I admit that it has ended up being one of the best things I've ever done? These women cheer me on, support me, tell me the hard stuff when I need to hear it, and make me stronger. I would like to believe they would say I do the same for them.

One really impactful example of this was that first year in Phoenix. That year was one of the loneliest I have had in my entire life. For the first time in eighteen years, I did not have a title or a position at a church. That was all I had ever known. I had grown accustomed to busy days full of prepping messages, empowering a staff, hanging on high school campuses, preaching, being creative, leading leaders, mentoring students ... and now here I was in a new city, in a new state, and there were no staff, leaders, students, no stage, no microphone, no big event to plan or message to prep. To be honest, I was lost. I wondered who I was outside of that role. I wondered what God was doing. I wondered what His plan was. I wondered what to do next. I didn't want my best years to be behind me.

Of course, being the self-reliant, pro-active person that I am, I tried to just start making things happen. What do I dream of? How could I accomplish that? What are the top ten ways to get there the fastest? With no thought to whether or not my position had changed, I barreled forward and tried to impress these people at the new churches we visited, our kids' new school, and the neighborhood. I wanted to show them who I was and what I was capable of. None of them knew much about me, let alone my track record. I felt I needed to prove my worth and fill the gaping void inside of me.

I started to sign up for things, serve wherever needed, and even launch a new ministry ... but nothing was feeling right. I had retreated right back to what I knew—a fast-paced, overcommitted, striving, proving mentality.

You see, I would post on social media about my "team brave" and our calls and how grateful I was for them, and women started reaching out, wanting to be part of this "thing." I saw a need. These women had the same desire that I did for community and authentic friendship. They wanted to be known, affirmed, and challenged, too. I recognized an opportunity when I saw it and thought: "This is it!" This was my chance to do "ministry." I could lead these women.

I shared this vision with my current team brave. Of course, they loved it. They were prepared to support me in any way that they could. I asked them what we should call it, and they all were adamant that it be called "team brave."

It was one thing for me to call my little tribe team brave, but to call a potential new movement that name would be another thing, completely. I explained to them that the phrase was coined by Jen DeWeerdt at the women's conference that had impacted me. In no way did I want to steal from what she created, and so I mentioned we would need to go another direction. But they disagreed.

I gave Jen a call to simply run it by her. Did she have a further vision for team brave? Did she plan to do anything with it? Or was it mainly for that one conference? We decided she should take a few days to think and pray about it, and she did. I truly wanted to honor her by taking her incredible idea further, and she honored me by encouraging me to go for it. I was so excited!

I began to dream and plan, and before long I had ideas for this potential team brave movement. Events, groups, gatherings ... live and online. Yes! Let's do it. Let's go.

I remember being on a call with two of my team brave members—Thea Wood and Jen Jones—and sharing about this event I wanted to hold but couldn't finish planning. The details wouldn't come together, and it all felt so difficult and forced.

On that call, Jen just said to me, "what are you really thinking right now? Do you feel like this is what God wants?"

I paused. It felt like a long time—and then I said, "No ... I actually don't. I think this may just be what I want."

So—I stopped the plans.

I pressed pause on MY plans.

I WENT BACK TO PURSUING GOD HIMSELF INSTEAD OF WHAT I COULD DO FOR HIM.

As much I was trying to avoid it, I knew that this next season was one when I needed to slow down and focus on my family, my marriage, and on me. To dive into what He already had given us, not on what I wanted to create. I went back to pursuing God Himself instead of what I could do for Him.

God's plan becomes evident when I plant myself in His promises, in His presence, and amidst Godly people. So this what I did.

So grateful for my team brave that day, and so many other days. The Zoom video calls. The text thread. The couple times a year we would actually get to see each other face to face. It may sound dramatic, but in some moments, they truly were a lifeline for me. A compass that would realign my direction and my dreams, helping me find true north.

If you really think about what Jeanne said, it is even research-backed that we become like the five people whom we spend the most time with. Who are your closest five? Do you really want to be like them? Do you want to parent like they do, step out in faith like they do, dream like they do, or love your husband and children like they do? Do they want what's best for you? Celebrate you, challenge you, support you?

If your vision of who these five should be differs from who your five actually are, it might be time to reevaluate your friends.

> *"Your circle should want to see you win. Your circle should clap loudly when you have good news. If it doesn't, get a new circle."*
>
> – Unknown

If you don't have these kinds of friendships, go find them! Pursue Godly, authentic friendships and create your own team brave. I had to do it. Is it easy? No way. It takes intentionality. It takes humility to step out and say, "hey, will you be my friend?" to someone whom you deeply admire. It takes time to prioritize each other. So easy? No. Worth it? Totally. It will change the quality of your life.

Some of us (my former self included) take for granted what we have, those opportunities we don't opt into: life groups, devo groups, women's nights, churches full of amazing women ... shame on us. If it's there and if it's being made available to you ... use it! Pursue it! If it's not available to you, then pray about creating it. Don't get too comfortable and settle into your friendships. Expand your circle.

"But, Megan, I don't have time to pursue friendships ..."

Stop it! You have time for whatever you want in life. We are better together. And we need each other.

So I would encourage you today to evaluate the key voices in your life as well as what you are doing with your own voice.

My personal goals are to have:

- Mentors in my life that I give permission to be honest with me
- Mentors that don't even know they are mentoring me through their books, podcasts and social media (people like Lysa TerKeurst, Christine Caine, Rachel Hollis, Ed Mylett, Brendon Burchard)
- Friends who are running this race alongside of me
- Girls younger than me who I am pouring into (and learning more about myself, as a result)

One of my favorite authors, Ann Voskamp, says, "*fear is what we feel—brave is what we do.*"

You may not feel brave, you may not feel courageous, but to be honest with you, it doesn't matter what you feel. It matters what you do.

So to sum it up my friends, I will leave you with this. Don't follow your heart. Lead it. Do not allow your emotions to have a say. Allow the purpose and dreams that God has placed within you to set your course. Live as if the Creator of the universe is by your side, leading you, guiding you, strengthening you, securing the path beneath your feet with every step, because He *is*. Fight for those friendships and to live your best life, even if you have to go through tough seasons in order to get there. May people see you pursuing God and saying yes to the adventure he has set before you and may they say ... SHE IS BRAVE.

CHAPTER FIVE

Season Of In-Between

"Learn how to honor the space between no longer and not yet."

– DANIELLE DOBY

Not long ago, I started to realize that my fuse was getting shorter and shorter. I'd get agitated quite easily and was definitely more anxious than usual. One night in particular, a few months ago, my heart was heavy. I could feel that dreaded lump-in-the-back-of-my-throat developing as the evening hours passed. The sensation was right there, begging to break through.

Tears welled up more than once, but I wasn't ready to give in or embrace that release, so I wiped my eyes, pushed the thoughts and emotional turmoil to the back of my head until I could get the kids settled and in bed (how many times do we mamas have to do that? Steel up! Brave face!)

Truthfully, what I wanted to do once I was finally off mom-duty for the night was to grab some ice cream, turn on Netflix, and scroll on Facebook. It's not rocket science at this point, but that would have been an obvious distraction to avoid thinking about what was truly happening with me. I even would have preferred to focus on menial tasks like cleaning the kitchen (which my husband definitely would have preferred). Any or all of those things would have been so much easier than intentionally pausing. Looking inward. Asking myself some honest questions and working to expose what was going on in my heart and mind.

It's embarrassing to admit, but I had slipped into a bad routine of numbing out, ignoring my emotions, and hiding myself in things I "needed" to do. Or I would just mask that twinge inside with a façade that everything was fine. Honestly, I thought I was doing everyone a favor and just, as they say, choosing joy—except when something small would happen, and anything *but* joy would spill out onto everyone I care about the most. I didn't realize how much I was doing that until a conversation with a counselor revealed that I had been stuffing and holding in a lot of things ... like—years' worth of things.

What a revealing conversation. It caused me to stop and reflect, and I was surprised to realize that he was spot on. I am typically a very authentic, vulnerable person. I would even consider myself a classic over-sharer and almost pride myself in being aware of and working through my issues.

Me? A stuffer? No!

And yet ... it was true.

Some pretty big events that had occurred in the last few years of my life and had brought about some very real and deep emotions in me. Yet—I just kept plugging along.

Classic Megan.

Stuff it. Cover it up. Avoid it.

Sometimes it feels like we women are supposed to be strong, right? We feel this unspoken, underlying pressure and expectation to keep it together for everyone else's sake. Maybe no one is saying it, but we imagine that they are thinking it? Maybe we are saying it to ourselves? Our husbands need us, our kids need us ... and they need us to be strong, right? As a result, sometimes out of a very well meaning heart, we make the choice to "keep it together" and kind of hope all the emotions will eventually sort themselves out.

I didn't want to burden those I loved. I wanted to be there for them. I just needed to work through my stuff on my own and move on. I don't recall a big moment where I made a conscious choice to close myself off or to keep things in—but after that very revealing conversation, I took an honest assessment of where I was at and why.

I had also made the recent decision to put a pause on creating a new ministry, starting a new movement, hosting events and forcing something that clearly wasn't working, as Jen and Thea had helped me realize. I had just laid down what I thought was a good idea and a God idea on the altar, meaning I surrendered it. Maybe later it would be the right time, maybe not. I didn't know. What I did know was that it was time to put less emphasis and energy on leading other people and ministries and start prioritizing leading myself in this new season. A healthier, happier me would affect everyone around me. I'd end up being a happier and healthier mom and wife, and my family would totally benefit from that.

Here is where I think many of us can get a little confused or disappointed: if something doesn't work out, our expectations aren't met, or if the doors don't open that we were hoping for, in our minds, we come to terms with the flashing red light. You know—the light that indicates apparently something isn't right. At least right now. So we stop. Or quit. Or even give up.

We sense the need to pause. Reassess. But definitely not to proceed.

Whatever.

But now what?

If not this, then what am I really supposed to be doing?

I have heard so many people say that they are waiting on God. But what does that look like? Waiting ... is it sitting on your rear end, waiting on Him to bring the answer or opportunity wrapped up in a box, tied with a pretty bow, and a list of instructions right to your doorstep, just like Amazon Prime?

Of course not! We say, but then all too often, we shut down or sit down and don't know what else we can do.

I was discouraged by the awareness that I was supposed to pause for a season, or at least what I hoped would only be a season. The reality is that I have been going, going, going for the last twenty years and have barely stopped to sit down. That is not a badge of honor; I know that. It is simply what I knew and had been doing. It felt right. It felt honorable. And so at that point, I didn't want to pause. Oh, man. I don't pause well. I didn't even really know what pausing looked like. I was convinced that I was ready for the next thing. I was willing! I was available! Why wouldn't God want to use me?

Heart excited, hand raised (put me in, Coach!), I felt like I had gotten benched. Hadn't I proven myself? Been faithful? Why not me? Why not now?

> *"Yet there is a difference between being buried and being planted. The difference is—when you plant a seed, you expect to see it rise again and come back to life ... When you go through tough times, you may feel like you've been buried, but the fact is, you've simply been planted. That means you're coming back. And you're not only coming back, you will come back better, increased, stronger."*
>
> – Joel Osteen (*It's Your Time*)

I'm reminded of a day years ago when Stasia came home with her little Mother's Day Styrofoam cup containing one little marigold flower. She was so excited to give it to me, and of course I thanked her and made a big deal about it. And so I planted it outside in a pot on the patio. Within a week or two, we were outside playing on the swing set with a few of the neighborhood kids. Before I even realized it, one ran over and plucked that one flower bloom right off the top of it. As if that wasn't enough, he demolished it right there in the dirt.

Of course Stasia was devastated. She cried; I comforted her, telling her it was going to be okay.

A week later, I walked outside, and a few marigolds were sprouting! The next time I noticed, even more had bloomed. And eventually, at least twelve little marigolds were sprouting. Though it had appeared that the flower died, in reality, it actually fertilized the ground and made it possible for even more to grow.

> *"Very truly I tell you, unless a kernel of wheat falls to the ground and dies, it remains only a single seed. But if it dies, it produces many seeds."*
>
> – John 12:24 (NIV)

Of course that's what God was doing to me. I wasn't being buried; he was planting me so that what I would turn into would produce tenfold what I had produced already.

I wish I would have realized that then, but learning it was part of the process.

As much as I hated those emotions I was feeling and dreaded hitting the pause button, I also had a peace that this was right. It just was. So I decided to take a season to do less talking and more listening. Less planning and more intentional space. And I hoped I would figure out what to do next.

"My heart is restless, O God, until it rests in Thee." – St. Augustine

STAYING BUSY ALLOWED ME TO AVOID THINKING ABOUT HOW I WAS REALLY DOING, AND PRAYING ABOUT OTHER PEOPLE ALLOWED ME TO AVOID LETTING GOD TELL ME HOW I WAS REALLY DOING.

My times with the Lord in that season had been filled with reading, study, and meditation. All the things you're supposed to do, right? But somewhere along the way, I had stopped journaling. My prayers prior to this time had been loud and long, but as of late—they had become short and quiet. Maybe even just a box to check off (truth). I prayed throughout the day, but they were pretty surface level prayers, and I often made them mostly about others. Staying busy allowed me to avoid thinking about how I was really doing, and praying about other people allowed me to avoid letting God tell me how I was really doing.

I recognize we all go through seasons spiritually, but I just don't think this was that. Over time I had unconsciously distanced myself from God, and like a shallow friendship, still showing up for coffee with Him and talking about the weather—what was going on around me—but avoiding what was going on inside me.

God has always loved me, you, all of us—broken. Just as we are. We don't have to fix ourselves for Him to love us. So why did I suddenly feel this need to be so put together? Since when had His love ever been conditional? Why did I feel like He would love me more if I were low-maintenance? ("Hey, God—how are things with you? Things are good here, thanks for asking. No really, I got this!")

I was discouraged that I felt like I was going backwards. Shouldn't I have been past these struggles of identity, rejection, self-reliance, and anxiety by now?

I knew all the answers to these questions in my head. It was time for a heart check, I guess.

Soon after, one night instead of Netflix or Instagram, I dug out a journal and sat down in the front room after the kids were all tucked in bed. I picked up the pen and finally put it back to paper. I struggled to find the words. I remember thinking, *I don't remember this being so hard*.

It was hard.

I chose in that moment to breathe in grace and to exhale perfection. I let go of the expectations I had for myself as well as the ones I felt others had for me.

I gave myself permission to be raw, weak, and undone. I began to write, scribbles across the pages of my journal, not like the author of a best-selling novel, but like my first grader:

"I feel sad right now. I talked to my dad tonight. I miss him. I miss my family so much. It's really hard being so far away. I feel lonely. Why do I feel so lonely? I feel guilty feeling these things, God. I have the best husband and kids. I have a beautiful home and amazing life. I don't want to take that for granted, but these feelings are real ... and I don't want to stuff them anymore."

I knew that's exactly what needed to happen right then. I needed to release my words to my Creator and not to anyone else. They were raw, and they were real.

The more I wrote, the easier it was. I didn't find a solution. In fact, I started writing about one burden and that literally led to another and another that I needed to write about ... I guess there was a lot brewing in there.

What I did discover in the midst of facing it all, instead of running from it all, was peace. I sensed "Emmanuel," another name for Jesus that means "God with us."

As my tears dropped onto the fresh ink of my journal pages, I felt very NOT alone. God met me there and tenderly reminded me to come just as I am and to receive the love that I don't deserve, but that I am worthy of because of Jesus.

How easy it is to forget that. That moment reminded me.

The in-between is just as important as any other season of life. Maybe more important is what we choose to do with that season when we are there.

I liken it to the cocoon—the caterpillar may not want to hang there either, but it is only the season in the cocoon that gives way to the ultimate metamorphosis. The process is hard. The middle is messy, but necessary. It is the evolution into all that caterpillar is meant to become and the ultimate birth of the beautiful butterfly.

I needed to allow myself to take a season to look inward instead of out. I made the decision to chase slow, to scale back, and to embrace the cocoon. To abide.

What does active abiding look like? It's not doing nothing; it's putting your energy into being faithful with what is in your hand, focusing on gratitude, sitting at His feet ... not striving, proving, or forcing momentum to get what you want (what if He wants something different? Even greater?).

In my decision to prioritize abiding, I committed to slow down and intentionally put more margin in my days, which was incredibly uncomfortable at first for me, someone who was used to going from one thing to another, normally running late and stressing about it. But when I left margin in my days, I had time and space—physically, mentally, and emotionally—to notice what kind of habits I had formed. The parts of my life which were unhealthy. To question my thought and habitual patterns and ask myself if they were true and were really serving me well, not to mention to consider how they were affecting those around me.

I had awareness and time to explore myself. Time for reflection and introspection. I started to look more deeply at what I was doing, saying, and being, and to consider whether it lined up with the deep desires of who I wanted to be and who I was created to be. Just because that was who I was then and had been for a long time didn't mean it was who I had to be moving forward.

JUST BECAUSE THAT WAS WHO I WAS THEN AND HAD BEEN FOR A LONG TIME DIDN'T MEAN IT WAS WHO I HAD TO BE MOVING FORWARD.

Have you ever been intentional to listen to yourself throughout the day or the week? Do you see patterns? Attitudes? Opinions? Things that are repeating again and again in your brain or are coming out of your mouth that you didn't even realize had become a part of your regular dialogue? What we say is a reflection of the beliefs in our hearts and minds. So what beliefs have formed that you may have unconsciously adopted over time? Are those things even true?

At my core I knew that my identity and purpose were not found in a title or position, but I started to realize based on my thoughts in this season that I didn't really believe that. I battled the lie that if I wasn't doing ministry and church activities that looked a certain way on a daily basis, and if I wasn't using the gifts I had previously used the way I was using them, I must be failing. Failing me, failing God, leaving an unfulfilled destiny.

Was this true based on the Word or through God's eyes? Of course not. But it was true in my world, and it had to be dealt with.

The problem with beliefs is that they affect everything—what we do, what we say, and decisions we make. As I became aware of this lie that I was believing, it was easy to recognize one of my core fears: "I don't matter." Similarly was the fear that "I'm not good enough." Partner those two, and you end up with a girl who does a lot of proving, striving, and chasing so that I can be sure to show the world and myself that those things aren't true.

I had pushed pause on volunteering for every one of my kids' activities and put launching a new ministry on hold. But the truth is that I was still looking over my shoulder at the past. What if my best days were behind me?

When we transitioned out of being pastors at the church to becoming full-time coaches with our health and hope ministry, I had mixed emotions. I was leaving behind my ministry and title. Would there really be room for me at a high capacity level in this new ministry? Everyone thought Dan was the rock star and honestly, he really was and still is. He is exactly where he is supposed to be, helping lead the international company and using his ministry and business gifts to impact the world at a global level. This is an answer to prayers I have prayed for years. Every day I am beyond grateful and humbled to be at his side.

This was the open door God had given us, and I knew it was right. I knew for sure I wasn't supposed to be launching the new ministry I had longed for. I wasn't sure what God was up to, but I opted to say yes and to trust Him. I decided that I would settle in to this place He wanted me to be now—mom for my kids, the business with my husband. I dove into building the business, which thank God, translated into helping people get healthy physically, emotionally, mentally, and financially, all of which were very life-giving.

Before long, I found myself scheduling check-ins, meetings, and trainings back to back to back. People were asking for my time, day and night. I was needed. I had purpose. I was making a difference. I realized quickly which activities got noticed and applauded. I found my avenue for affirmation, had opportunities to be in the spotlight, and was starting to feel "good enough."

One day, the fruit of my spirit and my life started to remind me that I was going back to my old ways. I was feeling hurried and stressed to fit everything in and get everything done, once again. I was struggling to make everyone happy. Those kids I had planned on giving so much focus to had gotten placed on the back burner once again and I knew—I knew that once again, something needed to change.

God had not called me into this season of abiding for me to just pick back up my habit of striving. Why could I just not get this figured out?! I found myself frustrated and disappointed with being back here once again. I found it crazy that we had moved across the country, new career, new community, new role ... same old habits. And I had learned this lesson already. Or so I had thought. Why was I prematurely trying to escape the cocoon when strength so often comes from the struggle?

GOD HAD NOT CALLED ME INTO THIS SEASON OF ABIDING FOR ME TO JUST PICK BACK UP MY HABIT OF STRIVING.

I began to realize that in order for me to coach others to be healthy, I needed to be healthy. I needed to "unbecome" the me I'd been for so many years. And I needed to abide in Him to start that process. He was the one, the only one, who could rebuild me.

I committed to the pause. The cocoon. I decided to change my morning routine, to really dig into the Word, to continue journaling. I started intentionally counting the gifts around me. I had to believe that He was orchestrating pieces and was going to bring it all together for something good.

As I started to do this, a funny thing happened. Things began to shift. I was experiencing more peace and joy. I started to realize how much I loved my life. I looked around me at all God was doing, in my marriage and our family, and found myself thankful and content. Not a contentment that indicates I was settling—but a genuine feeling of liking my life, feeling grateful for our home, our kids, and our business.

Maybe your life has turned out differently than you had planned or dreamed. That career you worked tirelessly for didn't pan out or wasn't what it appeared to be. So now you have student loans hanging over your head, a degree that you're not using ... what do you do with that? You may have a job that pays the bills but leaves you longing for fulfillment and purpose.

Or maybe that relationship you gave your heart to didn't work out. Maybe it seems like everyone around you is getting married (you're not) or has been married for a while.

Or it could be that you're married, and it's turning out to be far more difficult and way less glamorous than you expected—now that the Instagram wedding is over and the chaos and hardships of life have set in.

I know most assuredly that this book sits in the hands of many who gave it all they had, fought long and hard, but still find themselves devastated in the midst of a failed marriage.

Oh, you are not alone. Don't ever believe that you are.

Maybe parenting isn't anything you anticipated. It's so much harder than you imagined, and parenting absolutely reveals the mirror of who we are. Our kids repeat everything we say and suddenly—we need to revise. Oh, and what about that lie that parenting gets easier as they get older?! Tell me I am not the only one that got tricked by that thought!

Maybe you're a single mom (my heroes), and you shouldn't have to be going at this alone and wanting to do more than trying to make it through the day, running on empty. You wonder if anyone around you really understands where you are at and all that you have to do.

What about you who are struggling and disheartened because the fulfillment of your lifelong dream of motherhood seems like it may never become a reality ... at least not how you thought it would ...

If you find yourself one of the lucky few who, for the most part, has had a life that has been great, count your blessings. You have done the things you set out to do, but maybe even you, too, are growing restless because what once was enough isn't cutting it anymore. Maybe you just know there has to be something more.

Maybe it's a transition in life—a new job, the ending of an old job, moving to a new city or state, sending your last baby to kindergarten or off to college—suddenly, life is different.

It just is.

So, what now?

In these times we question whether something more is out there for us. And you may even feel guilty about it. You hesitantly hope that there is, but the fear that there isn't keeps creeping in. You often wonder if your best days are behind you.

These seasons of in-between are deceptive because they appear pretty unattractive. From the outside, they are often marked with times of loneliness, hopelessness, doubt, frustration, wandering, searching, waiting, longing, contending ... I mean let's get real, who wants to visit that place? Let alone move in for a while.

If you are like me, you would prefer to just skip that process. How about we just go right into inheriting and living the life of our dreams? We know God has a unique and good plan for each one of us, so why doesn't he just hand it to us? Why can't our prayers just be answered according to our timing and God allow the path to be smooth and effortless?

Have you heard what happens to the butterflies that are rescued prematurely? If we were to see what appears to be the discomfort of the cocoon, the wiggling, the struggle, and try to rescue that butterfly by opening the cocoon from the outside, what would happen?

I'll tell you what would happen. That butterfly would not survive. Because it is in the process of the struggle that that butterfly gains the strength it will need not only to survive in this season, but also to thrive in the next. We can't rush that process. Not with caterpillars, butterflies ... and most certainly, not with us.

We gain strength through the struggle, and it is because we have persevered and refused to give up that we are able to become all we were meant to be ...

I believe there are millions of women who are trying to avoid or skip over the process of the cocoon instead of embracing what God wants to do in that season of in-between.

I was!

But I had to travel through that season. There was no way I could be there for my family unless I got healthier emotionally, mentally, and spiritually. I made an intentional decision not to just *go* through this season, but also to *grow* through it. This was going to be a journey of trust and faith, even when I couldn't see what God was doing.

How many of us are still walking around as caterpillars when deep in our hearts and souls we just know we were always meant to be butterflies?

I will warn you, friend, the cocoon is not for the faint of heart. But I will also tell you that WE CAN DO HARD THINGS.

> *"Just when the caterpillar thought her life was over, she began to fly."*
>
> – Barbara Haines Hewitt

The season of in-between is not easy, but it sure is worth it. How do I know? Because I have been there. It's unlike anything I have ever experienced, and I am so thankful for it, now.

> *"Abiding informs calling. When your activity ends, His begins."*
>
> – Rebekah Lyons

This is exactly what I experienced. When I stopped, He started. My only action was to abide.

John 15:4–8 says, "*Abide in Me, and I in You. As the branch cannot bear fruit of itself, unless it abides in the vine, neither can you, unless you abide in Me. I am the vine, you are the branches. He who abides in Me, and I in him, bears much fruit; for without Me you can do nothing. If you abide in Me, and My words abide in you, you will ask what you desire, and it shall be done for you. By this My Father is glorified, in that you bear much fruit; so you will be My disciples.*"

I needed God to put me back in my place. He is the vine and I am the branch. Nothing (that matters or has lasting impact) happens apart from Him. And I love how it says that our Father is glorified when we bear much fruit. It is His desire that we fulfill our purpose and do great things. But what if that happens not by what we accomplish and more by who we become?

When I took my rightful place, I moved from the verb *wonder* (desiring, wanting and curious to know something or to doubt) to a place I would much rather be ... experiencing the noun *wonder* (a feeling of surprise mingled with admiration, caused by something beautiful, unexpected, unfamiliar, or inexplicable.)

I couldn't think of a better way to describe that time in the cocoon: surprise mingled with admiration, caused by something beautiful, unexpected, and unfamiliar.

CHAPTER SIX

Becoming

"There is a season for wildness and a season for settledness and right now is neither. This season is about becoming."

– SHAUNA NIEQUIST

I could already sense that my season of abiding was creating things inside me to shift in a positive way: the commitments I had made—a more intentional morning routine, leaning into what I was truly feeling, paying attention to it and the way that it affected me. I was actually trying to implement a tool that we use with all of our clients: "Stop. Challenge. Choose." I have previously allowed the fact that I am a passionate person to be an excuse to react emotionally or quick-wittedly, even if it was really a defensive or protective move. It was time to stop that. I lacked a ton of self-control in many areas, and this tool really assisted me to pause, think about what I want most, and then make my choice.

I may want to tell my husband off when he pushes my hot buttons and prove him wrong, but ultimately more than that, I care about our relationship, so my response needs to reflect that.

I may feel hurt or defensive about someone's criticism of me, but ultimately I desire to be the best me, so I am going to choose to assume the best about them and take the nugget of truth from what they said and use it to make me better.

I may be frustrated with my kids' choices or lack of respect, but if my goal is for them to really understand why something is so important to me, I will take the time to sit down and explain it in a tone that they can hear versus responding in a way that shuts them down.

I may invite someone to coffee (a few times) and they may decline, forget, or cancel at the last minute, but instead of taking it personally, I give them the grace I would like to receive and send an invitation out to a few others.

I still have a long way to go, but this one practice was altering things tremendously for me. "Stop. Challenge. Choose." Thank you, Dr. Wayne Andersen, the founder of our company, for mentoring me and believing I absolutely have the ability to become the best me, and that it's never too late for a person to change his or her mind and life.

I was spending more time in the Word, praying, and journaling, and it wasn't because I needed to speak on Wednesday or prep for a leaders' meeting. It was because I wanted to know God more, and I needed his wisdom for my life. I was beginning to see old patterns start to fall to the wayside and felt freedom was on the horizon.

Yet—I knew there was more to do. The newfound peace and gratitude I was feeling for my life indicated that I was heading in the right direction, but I had a hunger to be healthy and grow by leaps and bounds in ALL aspects of my life.

Right around this time, my oldest daughter, Mariah, was approaching her first football game as a cheerleader. She had done tumbling and cheer sporadically growing up and been invited to join a gymnastics travel team up north, but with our crazy family and ministry calendar, I thought—no way. Not gonna lie—I may have strongly encouraged her to do another sport, any other sport, and she went on to try and excel at them all, too ... soccer, basketball, volleyball ... but she was always drawn back to tumbling.

We finally agreed to enroll her at a gym when we moved to Phoenix. This girl is a hard worker. I mean fierce. When she wants something, she is willing to do anything to get it. By her own determined choice to do her part to save the animals, she went vegetarian at the age of ten. Despite my doubts and speculations, she never went back! In fact, she later became a vegan at the age of 13.

Mariah would go to the gym and do the work, then exercise and practice more at home. When she made the school cheerleading squad, the workload for her increased, but she took it in stride: more practicing, more time committed, up late at night to finish homework—we clearly had found one of her passions.

The first football game was on the horizon. The maiden voyage of her new role was fast approaching. She had done all the work leading up to it and was more than ready.

Mere days before, she and a friend were stunting at our house, and out of nowhere, I heard shrill screams—the kind that any mom knows they don't want to hear. "MOM! (scream), MOM! (scream), MOM! Hurry!"

I ran to the front room where Mariah was cradled on the floor. Now, we are talking, this is my tough-as-nails kid. Even so, she looked up at me, tears streaming down her face, and said "Mom, my knee. I got hurt. I am not okay."

I immediately knew it was serious.

I looked down and tried to not show emotion, but I mean, yeah—it was beyond clear in my split-second look that she had, without a doubt, dislocated her knee—it just looked "off." Trying not to freak out, but doing a terrible job, I ran to get Dan to figure out what to do. When we got back (like 30 seconds later), my girl had put her kneecap back in place. I am totally serious. (Let's be real ... I would not have touched a thing and just kept crying). Who was this incredible person we had created?

While all this was happening, Mariah's little BFF had called 911 ... I mean, can you see how dramatic this event was? I said "Ava, it's all right. Tell them we don't need them and are headed to urgent care." You've got to love her make-it-happen efforts. In the end, Dan carefully carried her to the car, I drove to urgent care, and they came out to get her and wheel her in. They proceeded to tell me that her quick and brave response to put her knee back in place was the best action she could have possibly taken, and that the more time it was out of place, the more damage could have been done (let's pause and remember this because we are going to come back to it).

They wrapped her up, told us to head home, elevate and ice it, and get to the orthopedic doc as quickly as we could. Long story short, my tough girl was now on crutches, and I was scared to death any time she moved, as they had casually mentioned that because this happened, it was more likely the kneecap could slip again. I obviously did NOT want that to happen. So I kept the ice coming and forced her to elevate and proceed with any caution if she was going to move or had to go up the stairs or really do anything.

"Mariah! Are you icing that knee like I told you to?"

To say she was disappointed wouldn't come close to how she was feeling. My mama heart broke for her. After a visit to the ortho, x-rays and a consult, they suggested physical therapy, but warned us that if this continued to be a problem, she may need surgery. Say what?! Ugh. I started to ask around about physical therapy offices and see what our options were.

Meanwhile, the coach wanted her to come to attend the first game anyway, as a member of the squad. She did. She sat and watched like she got benched, but through no one's fault, in particular. Certainly not hers.

I will never forget a certain moment in the physical therapy room with her. I had been telling her to elevate her leg, to ice it, to make sure it was still (no movement!) and not allow it to get further irritated.

To my surprise, at the first session the therapist quickly informed me that all of those things are some of the biggest mistakes people make.

Perfect. "Mom of the Year" award again goes to me. The Villain.

The therapist explained how "being still" is a very common misconception. She expressed that *healing comes through motion*. Don't freeze your motion, don't ice your injury, don't nurse that wound. You've got to get back out there and get that muscle going again and strengthen it. You have to keep it moving, keep it flexible, preserve the muscle memory of what is already known.

She also explained how many career-ending injuries end the way they do because many athletes have the mindset of "that really hurt. I'm not going to risk that again."

Mariah turned to look at her after she said that and raised her eyebrows slightly, saying confidently, "Well, that's not me. Tell me what I need to do to get back out there." Yup. That's our girl!

Mariah ended up having to do months of physical therapy. It was so much work; she had all these little exercises she had to do at home; she had to change the way she did certain things, all because she wanted to get out on the field and do what she loved. There was a clear end goal that my girl wanted to achieve.

The day she prepared to tumble again (meaning she had to rely on that knee to land), she faced another mental challenge. After a number of starts and stops, her therapist looked at her and said, "Take off the brace."

She did. Mariah kept hesitating, but the fear was messing with her and holding her back.

Dr. Sara then said, "You're going on three, or we're done for today."

"One—two—three—go!!"

Mariah took off and did it! That first time granted her the confidence to keep going, and she is now an all-star competitive cheerleader with one of the top teams in the country! You would never know she had that injury as she now completes these tumbling passes, flipping from one side of the gym to the other. I always talk about her fearless spirit, but honestly—that doesn't give her the credit for the fear she had to face and overcome to create that brave spirit within her. I am overjoyed that she has developed this grit at such a young age.

"Healing comes through motion."

"Don't freeze it; don't ice it."

"The longer it's out of place and you nurse the wound, the more damage there will be."

All of these lines from the PT stuck with me. I couldn't get away from them. I could see so clearly the correlation of what Mariah was going through physically with what I was going through emotionally. I knew I needed to apply that theory to my current place in life. I was abiding, I was improving, but how could I find motion and healing in a season of pause?

That's when I recognized the next level of heart work and hard work I had to do. God was saying, "I have you where I have you for a reason. If I want you somewhere else, I'll take you there, but right now I need you to do the work."

One of the most important first steps for me at this stage of becoming who I wanted to be was to decide to go to counseling. Firsthand, I saw the power of Mariah having a coach, a therapist, someone from the outside with an unbiased view who solely was in it for her benefit. Someone who knew what she wanted and what it would take for her to get there and was willing to say the hard stuff, push her in a healthy way, and challenge her fears and anything else holding her back. Admittedly, I played this role for many people but didn't have someone doing this for me. It was time. I knew I needed a safe place to open up, work through "stuff," and receive spiritual and practical guidance.

These sessions allowed me to release all that I had been holding in.

Often, I just needed to be asked a few questions, talk it all out, cry it all out, and hear myself admit where I really was. I didn't need answers. I just needed to get it out. I had so many awakenings as I listened to the completely vulnerable and unfiltered me. I could be honest about my buried anger and resentment that were uncovered in these sessions. I could own it.

I could admit the fact that my expectations of what this season looked like weren't being met and how it was disappointing and hurtful. My counselor encouraged me that since I couldn't change anyone else, maybe it would serve me better to change my expectations (truth bomb). I shared about the paralyzing anxiety I was fighting because I felt like things were so out of control. And I learned about controlling what I could (myself), and to quit trying to control what I couldn't (other people and situations).

SINCE I COULDN'T CHANGE ANYONE ELSE, MAYBE IT WOULD SERVE ME BETTER TO CHANGE MY EXPECTATIONS.

I needed someone to affirm that I had God-given needs of affirmation, community and the desire to be known, but also to look at me and tell me to stop looking for my husband or others to meet those needs. It was my job to get those needs met. First through God, but then by joining a Bible study, and also strategically planning coffee appointments and relational connection times, because I used to have that but didn't in this season. I needed someone other than my husband to ask me if a martyr or victim mentality—the belief that things were happening TO me instead of FOR me—was assisting me to go where I wanted to go and be who I wanted to be.

Because as much as I was ready to move on from the past and to let go of any old baggage I was still carrying, I walked right into another season that provided many opportunities to pick up offense, anger, and hurt. Dan's dad had passed away and his brother, in spite of the love and many forthright honest interventions, including a ridiculous confrontation by me in a parking lot where I lost it on him, spiraled back on a path of addiction and fraud. He landed himself back in jail, leaving four kids (with three different moms) behind, for the next eight years.

I feel a responsibility to help, but I can only do so much. Even now, I sit here in tears as I type this, about eighteen months into his sentence, because of how hard this has been on everyone. I so badly want to forgive him and have so many times. But addiction is hard. It's really hard when people don't take personal responsibility. And it's hard to look at these kids and try to help them understand that they are known and loved and wanted when they feel anything *but*. It's hard and sometimes inconvenient to coordinate and help raise another kid almost every weekend, yet so wonderful and rewarding at the same time.

The anger comes in waves, and it's hard. It's hard when Dan's brother calls and he feels great because he talked to his kid. I do respect the effort that he's making, but it's really hard when you are the one that has to hold the crying child after each phone call because he's eight and his emotions are big and real and not going away anytime soon.

Are you hearing me? LIFE IS HARD sometimes. I get it. We can do everything we know to live our best lives possible, and other people's choices still have the ability to mess it up. It is what is, and as much as I want to, I can't fix it or change the situation. I can only do the work to be the best me, the best wife, mom, aunt, coach, etc. ... That is what I CAN do.

> *"Do not fast forward into something you are not ready for,*
> *or allow yourself to shrink back into what's comfortable.*
> *Growth lives in the uneasiness.*
> *The in between.*
> *The unfinished sentence*
> *You are a season of becoming."*
>
> – Danielle Doby

Who did I want to become? It was time to get clear on that and what it would take and start to honor those commitments to myself. It was time to stop focusing on outside circumstances and start looking within.

- If I wanted to be a great friend and have great friends, I'd have to continue things like my team brave. I'd have to reach out to new people in my city, make time for coffee or lunch, and prioritize reaching out instead of waiting for my phone to ring.

- If I wanted to be a great wife, what did that look like? What did I need to do to make that happen?
- If I wanted to make a difference in my kids' lives—same questions!
- I was already focusing on the inner work by changing habits and going to a counselor. I was becoming self-aware enough to realize things like when I was yelling at my kids too much. I recognized when I was numbing out at night rather than dealing with these feelings like I had in the past and begin to operate at a higher level.
- Through the heart work of journaling and the other things I had been doing while in that cocoon phase, I realized the patterns in me that I previously blamed on others and over which I had to start taking ownership. It was at this time that I felt a turning point from being the villain to leaning into what this heroine could be. This was my life, and I myself was ready to take responsibility for what I was allowing and creating.
- It became very obvious that if I were going to create motion while abiding, I needed to be my very best version of me—healthy in all aspects—mentally, emotionally, physically, and spiritually.

I moved forward on the physical side of health. For years, I had put myself at the bottom of the list in this area, mainly because I felt I didn't have the time and I knew we were so strapped financially. I needed some serious dental work done. I simply hadn't made it a priority. We were paying for other things. I had health issues that had been nagging at me for years, so many that I am even still taking care of some of them, but after watching Mariah's strength and determination, I began to "create motion," making much-needed appointments with doctors, dentists, and surgeons. I, too, wanted to be healthy enough to be able to get back in the game if the coach called me up. I wanted to feel good enough to be the kind of wife and mom that was fun and fully present.

I began to choose to add more reading to my life, more leadership, spiritual, and personal development podcasts rather than mindlessly scrolling my phone and zoning out. The truth is that many of these decisions were very small things to change, but the sum of all parts was adding up to a much healthier Megan.

As a slight aside during this chapter on health ... if you are like most people I know, this would be an easy chapter to turn the page to skip right over, but your calling, that dream in your heart—look, it means too much. Your marriage, your kids, the legacy you are leaving, the chance to raise kids who are going to follow the dream in their hearts means too much to turn the page on this topic that is often too taboo for even many churches to really address. Why is that?

I know a lot of unhealthy pastors and church people. It's because I can recognize the signs. My husband and I were some of these people for years and years.

Unfortunately, as pastors, we were teaching from the Word and offering people a life of freedom from shame and guilt, empowering them to live an abundant life. Meanwhile, we had zero control or freedom in the area of physical health ourselves. We were preaching to people to make Jesus Lord of their lives, and then we personally were hand-picking the areas in our lives in which we actually let him have a say. Ouch. Stepping on your toes? Sorry! (Not sorry). Trust me—mine were stepped on first. But honestly, I'm so grateful. You and I both know that He desires to be Lord of all. *All.*

This is why it's hard for me to understand why so many people don't address this topic or just won't go there. I know it can be hard and we fear offending people and it's easier to be politically correct. We as the church are willing to offend people about other areas of their lives if they aren't in line with the Word, but so often, not this one. Why?!

It's undoubtedly hard to live and to lead in today's world with everyone hanging on so tightly to their right to do what they want, or be what they want. If someone doesn't support or agree with you, that person is seemingly wrong and made to be the bad guy (Side note: I'm not the bad guy ... don't kill the messenger. Don't send me a mean email; just ask yourself why you're upset and take it to the Lord. I have enough drama with my teenage and almost teenage girl at home. I don't need any more! Plus let's be honest ... you don't even want to see the number of unread emails in my inbox).

We all battle the need to be politically correct and avoid being offensive. And then we so easily find ourselves on the defense. Let's shift things for a minute. What if we as people were less easily offended? Not so sensitive? What if we were more open and desiring to be coached and led?

I, myself, had to learn this concept and develop the desire to be open to hearing things about myself I might not like. I just shared with you how long it took me to learn to stop striving so hard. But here was the conclusion that I came to: we have ONE LIFE, one shot at this ... our quality of life and even our length of life will be affected by what we choose to do in this area of our lives—physical health. If I have any ounce of real love for you, then we need to go there. If I'm wrapped up in myself and worried about offending you, then I won't do it.

So here we go ...

My husband and I were busy doing God's work, true, but aren't we each individually God's handiwork and masterpiece? We were not being good stewards of that. We were not stewarding our temples (bodies) or our talents well. My husband was 80 pounds overweight. I had a little weight to lose, but for me it was the low energy, sugar addiction, high inflammation, heartburn, and other issues I was experiencing. Both of us were seeing how these afflictions were affecting our marriage and our kids. We were not being the best spouses or parents, and we knew it. It's hard to look into the mirror sometimes.

I remember so clearly the beautiful spring day that my husband went out to jump on the trampoline with my kids. He came back in about five minutes later, huffing and puffing and looking at me with sheer panic in his eyes. He literally thought he was having a heart attack. He genuinely began to fear that if he stayed on his current trajectory that he wouldn't be around to walk our daughters down the aisle. This is when he had to start asking himself what he wanted most.

Drive-thrus, though convenient, pizza and tacos, though tasty—none of them were worth losing what was most important ... being able to run and play with our kids now and be here decades later with us still enjoying life. We had been making the wrong choices.

Jesus died to give us the abundant life—but our physical health was holding us back from that. We were not living a fully abundant life. Is that the life you are living?

Hear me out ...

It's not about how we look ... let's explore that ... yes, outer beauty fades ... it's not where we should invest all our time and energy ... that should be our character and our calling. But aren't confidence, peace, joy, love, and self-control part of our character, and aren't those affected when we are unhealthy or overweight? How could they not be? Aren't our relationships affected when those areas of our lives are not in a good place? When we don't have the energy to do what we feel God has created us to do, or be the mom or wife we want to be? Is that really the life God desires for us? Is it even the life we desire for ourselves?

I work with moms all the time who tell me, "yeah, it's all good. I just need to lose 20, 40, however many pounds."

But listen. It's not about getting fixated on a number on a scale. It's about freedom to be the best you and live the highest quality and longest life possible. What would be different in your life if you woke up tomorrow and that 20–30 pounds were gone?

"Oh my gosh!" They tell me. "I would be able to walk in my closet and pick out whatever clothes I want; I wouldn't overthink it or spiral emotionally into shame or frustration because I don't have anything that fits and feel terrible about it."

Awesome. What else?

"I would have the energy to take my kids to the park and chase after them! I wouldn't think twice about taking them to the pool! I would get in pictures with them and make more memories with them. I wouldn't feel guilty about the example I'm being to my daughter. I tell her to smile, be confident, be bold, to be herself, not to care what people think. But I struggle with all that myself."

How would it affect your relationships with others?

"I wouldn't spend so much time comparing myself, feeling jealous or insecure, bad about myself."

Your marriage?

"I would feel confident and sexy. My husband would be happy, not because he thinks I need to change—he says he loves me how I am and I look good—but I don't believe him because I don't even like looking in the mirror and affects how I show up (or don't actually) in the bedroom."

My conversation about health with most women, wives, and moms starts with them being very unsure if they have the time or money to invest in getting healthy. They struggle with the idea that it's selfish to invest in themselves but quickly, as our conversation evolves, it becomes apparent that what equates to a woman getting healthy is that her kids get a better mom, husband gets a better wife, and friends get a better friend. And that actually, if they were healthy, they would have so much mental,

emotional and physical freedom that their time an
would now be focused on others instead of themselv

Health isn't just about losing weight; it's about handing over control. It's about putting food back in its rightful place in your life. And God in His. Food is simply meant to be our fuel, what energizes us for the mission. Not our best friend or comfort or entertainment. Where do you go when you're stressed? When you're sad? Can you attend events, parties, and dinners with people and it be about the people and not the food?

HEALTH ISN'T JUST ABOUT LOSING WEIGHT; IT'S ABOUT HANDING OVER CONTROL.

What's amazing is that when we make a decision to pursue health, it immediately flows over into other areas of our lives! We can't start trying to focus on our nutrition without dealing with our thoughts and mindsets and habits that arise in the process. When we are empowered by our choices instead of battling shame, we want more of that! We want self-control, a higher quality of life mentally, spiritually, relationally, and financially.

It is a choice, maybe one that seems difficult at first, and then we wonder why we ever waited to do it in the first place.

That's kind of where I was. I was putting things into motion, taking back my health in all of these areas, and I learned that you can't just try to change a bad habit. You have to replace it.

As a new entrepreneur, I learned quickly how unorganized I was and how easily time was wasted. I knew to become the best me I would need to embrace structure as my new best friend in this season and moving forward.

By nature, I rebel against structure. I like to think I am wild and free, which seems like #goals ... but then the week goes by, and I have accomplished nothing I intended to and am no closer to reaching my goals. I've leaned towards having a plan and watching that plan get thwarted as I would react based on emotions or feelings or other people.

In a season like this, the entire time period can be very emotional. Please understand that you can't trust your emotions in transitional seasons. I was Unbecoming, and then Becoming, and it was so emotional. Not to mention, I was battling early menopause and dealing with unbalanced hormones due to some of the health issues I mentioned. I couldn't follow my heart; I had to lead it. I had to put structure and discipline into my life and absolutely follow that structure. This included everything from saying, "I don't have time for date night this week" and then absolutely adhering to the structure of keeping date night because I valued my marriage, to making sure that each Sunday, I planned out our family's weekly schedule so that ideally, nothing would catch us by surprise.

I watched as structure started reshaping my life.

Another tool I incorporated into my life was taking time in the morning to write out my goals as if they had already happened. Here's an example of what I write often:

I only have one life to live and only one (today's date) and I will live it to the full with no regrets.

1) *I am a fun, fabulous, and fully-present mom.*
2) *I am a kind, supportive, and sexy wife.*
3) *I am a daughter of God and I love to make him smile.*
4) *I pursue my Creator daily, hungry to grow, learn, and walk in obedience to the call on my life.*
5) *I organize and center my life around what matters most to me: faith, family, purpose, and legacy.*
6) *I am a hope dealer and have a solution for a hurting world and will offer it boldly and in love.*

7) *I am a speaker of life, love, and what's to come.*
8) *I fuel my body and eat according to my goals.*
9) *I exercise and grow stronger every day.*
10) *I am a coach that empowers others to live their best lives and I lead by example.*
11) *I bring value every day on social media and in person.*
12) *I am an author. My story matters, and someone needs to hear it.*
13) *I contribute my time, talent, and resources to make my community/world a better place and to build the kingdom of God.*
14) *I don't live for the temporary, but for the eternal.*

This is my opportunity to get clear on my goals and my purpose. Reminder: the power is in writing them daily, reading them out loud, and then asking the question, "What am I going to do today to prove these things true or make them a reality?" Be intentional to break down your big goals into small ones, translate them into actual items in your calendar, and then be sure to show up. I would never say I was going to meet someone and then just not show up. I had to learn to give myself and my goals the same respect I gave to everyone else and theirs.

I HAD TO LEARN TO GIVE MYSELF AND MY GOALS THE SAME RESPECT I GAVE TO EVERYONE ELSE AND THEIRS.

If I'm a fully-present mom, that means when I pick my kids up, no phone.

If I'm a kind wife, I don't allow myself to go below the line and get short or disrespectful to my husband ... and if I do I recognize it, own it, and apologize.

If I am a sexy wife, it means I make an effort to take care of myself, be confident, and show up that way. This takes intentionality when I am tired or when my hormones are a hot mess.

(In case I don't have another chance to mention it ladies ... please get your hormones checked, get some blood work done, and see where you may be deficient. Sometimes we make our issues mental/emotional when they are physical and could be adjusted.)

If I am committed to use my time, talents, and resources for the good of my community and the Kingdom of God, I need to pray and decide where I am going to commit those things and then honor those commitments and feel empowered saying no to things outside of those.

This list is a recognition of who I want to be. It guides me in making intentional choices each day to make that a reality.

That in-between season, the cocoon, that two years of abiding and becoming ... all of that was still in effect. I was putting myself into motion and doing the hard work, like I watched Mariah do. Healing comes from motion. I was replacing the bad habits with great habits, and my lens of life had turned into gratitude.

One morning, I went into our front room with my big, hot pink Message Bible. I sat down and just took a breath and looked around me before I opened it. The sun was slanting in through the shades, it was quiet, and I was at peace. I realized just how happy I was there in Phoenix. It had nothing to do with the geographic location. It had everything to do with becoming. I had desperately needed to become who I was supposed to be. I just started to tell God how grateful I was for what I had in my hand rather than wishing for what I used to have in my hand or needing to know what would come next. I knew that He had been transforming me, and as a result, I had a deep satisfaction.

After a few minutes, I opened my Bible to this passage:

"You're blessed when you're content with just who you are—no more, no less. That's the moment you find yourselves proud owners of everything that can't be bought."

– Matthew 5:5 (MSG)

Such a confirmation for me. I had let Him be enough. I had let me be enough. I didn't need all the "more"—all the extra. There was such victory in that.

In the same moment, I felt a strong release from Him. I knew He was telling me, *this is where I wanted you to get to, dependent and content in Me. Now you're in a place where you can go forward. I didn't call you to the "less-than" life. There is more.*

Wait! Hold up just a second.

I had just found all the gratitude and contentment! I liked my life! I liked where I was. I had found my rhythm and my hiking and my water intake and my coffees with friends (counselor recommended). I was putting into practice all of these things and structure and creating joy all around me. I was leveling out my hormones and noticing a difference. I loved coaching alongside my husband and getting opportunities to travel and train leaders with him. I could finally get back to my house without using the map on my phone—NOW you want to pull me off the bench and put me back into the game?

Even though I always knew there was more, I didn't feel that release in the previous season. I had to take that personal journey. I had to be faithful in the in-between. I had to be committed to becoming because the person I was when I left the last season was not someone who could accomplish what He had for me in the next season. I had to unpack and Unbecome in order to Become so I could be the person that He needed for what was ahead.

I had pushed pause, surrendered those dreams, not knowing if that release would ever come. I had told God that I felt like there were these women all around me who were crying out for mentorship and community, leadership and empowerment. But seriously—I knew there was work to be done there.

On the other hand, I didn't want to go back to my old habits. I didn't want to strive again. This was really a test of motives because I did not want it to be about me. Before, I had wanted this so badly, almost needed it, and it didn't work. This time, I wasn't longing for it at all. In fact, I had fallen in love with the slower life, this time of hibernation and healing. It had done me so much good, and I wasn't convinced I wanted to step out again.

Yet I felt Him encouraging me, nudging me that this time it wasn't about me. It was his desire. It would be an act of obedience to step out of the comfort zone I had recently gotten settled into. He was calling me forward.

I got off the bench, a bit guarded and a bit hesitant, but ready to go in.

CHAPTER SEVEN

Pursuit

"This is the season she will make beautiful things. Not perfect things but honest things that speak to who she is and who she is called to be."

– MORGAN HARPER NICHOLS

I don't know if you've ever played sports. I played a few growing up, and I can remember that specific moment when the coach would turn, look at me, and say, "You're going in!"

As a player, you want that moment. It's what you have been waiting for. You long to be able to get in there and prove your worth, that you're good enough. You want to enjoy the game, not as a spectator from the sidelines, but as part of the team out in the field (or in the pool since I was a swimmer). *Put me in, Coach!*

But you also have that slight sensation of ... *can I really do this? Do I have what it takes?*

My pink Bible moment was calling me off the bench. And while I desired to obey what God was whispering in my heart to do, the crazy thing was ... I didn't really want all that anymore.

I had previously wanted a ministry of my own, volunteer work that kept me super busy and involved, and any dots on my iCal that would make me feel like I was "doing something." Like I was important and needed.

But then I paused.

I abided.

I went through The Becoming.

And I got to the point where I didn't need all of that anymore. Not like I used to, anyway. It didn't mean I didn't love some of that stuff. Or that it didn't make me come alive. But I didn't crave it, or mourn it or feel incomplete without it any longer.

I had done the hard work. I had done the heart work. And was still doing it because it isn't a one and done type deal. It's this ongoing process of keeping myself in check or losing it and then refocusing. Getting off course and then taking aim once again. But I will say that this season (now going on for years, by the way, just in case you were likening this season to, oh—say fall or winter or something—no, I am not talking a few months) was totally transforming the way I viewed my life, my calling, and my work.

I felt like I had just settled in, was feeling comfortable, and now God was calling me to get back out there? I had worked so hard to get to the point where the external factors didn't matter as much and I wasn't striving to create something for myself that when the God release happened, I got a little uneasy.

It took me a little bit to figure out ... why the hesitation? What was the struggle? I realized that my fear was no longer of potential failure. It was of success.

Wait, what? Who fears success?

That was an indicator to me that my motives were on the right track, but what else was that telling me? I wasn't afraid of failing and having people judge me. To be honest, I had grown to have such high esteem for those people that were just willing to put themselves out there and go for it regardless of the result. Over those last four years, my measuring stick of what failure and success looked like had truly shifted.

As for me personally, I was afraid of succeeding in a way that might change me. How that might affect my family, our calendar, or my availability to be present for those whom I love the most?

I had really grown to love the fact that my husband and I worked for ourselves and that our business was now at the place that we could do what we wanted, when we wanted, and work from wherever. Trust me, I was truly enjoying this newly found time and financial freedom that we had never had before. I could make work calls on-the-go, show up and be field trip mom, meet up with my husband for a day date or a friend for coffee. My husband and I could pick up and travel on our own or with the kids if we felt like it. Did I really want more potential commitments? Calendar events to lock me in?

When I started this journey four years ago, I was unsure of how to handle the open time in my days. Now, I cherished it. I had grown to love solitude, trying new things and living life on my terms. I had been re-introduced to parts of me that had gone missing and was enjoying discovering parts of myself that I never knew were there (like a love for cowboy boots and country music).

I had grown really content and comfortable. Maybe too comfortable.

> *"Disturb us, Lord, when we are too well pleased with ourselves,*
> *when our dreams have come true because we have dreamed too little,*
> *when we arrive safely because we sailed too close to the shore.*
> *Disturb us, Lord, when with the abundance of things we possess,*
> *we have lost our thirst for the waters of life,*
> *having fallen in love with life, we have ceased to dream of eternity,*
> *and in our efforts to build a new earth,*
> *we have allowed our vision of the new heaven to dim.*
> *Disturb us, Lord, to dare more boldly, to venture on wider seas,*
> *where storms will show your mastery,*
> *where losing sight of land, we shall find the stars.*
> *We ask you to push back the horizon of our hopes,*
> *and to push us into the future in strength, courage, hope, and love."*
>
> – Sir Francis Drake

This pink Bible moment ... that verse in Matthew ... were really leaving me disturbed. Was I ready?

For years I spoke from stages, coached leaders, and preached sermons. But I had changed. My relationship with God and the Bible had changed and evolved. I felt healthier than ever, but I also wasn't sure that I wanted to get back out there (side note: to me, healthy doesn't equate to having arrived—it more so means that I am growing in self-awareness and making deliberate choices to become the best version of myself). I was more aware of my issues and imperfections than ever. Sure, I battled feeling "qualified" to get out there and speak and lead others. But since I was young, I have trekked through the Bible and have known that God doesn't choose the qualified. He chooses the willing.

Gulp.

Was I willing?

My desire had always been for God to use me to make a difference in the lives of others. But I honestly wasn't sure that I wanted to sign back up for leadership or the spotlight. The truth was, we hadn't gotten away from leading others—we did so in our business and with our coaching team daily, but spiritual leadership? Whew! That was different. It seems to come with so much pressure, even if it's just self—induced. I didn't want to put myself back in a glass house. I have an amazing family and the most incredible and sexy husband, but even after seventeen years together, we are so far from perfect.

Confession: We had family drama this morning ... like the ungrateful kids annoying each other and being inconsiderate and pushing each other's buttons which then pushes our buttons until someone just blows up type of drama. I know you get it. My tear-stained face and puffy red eyes as I sit here typing this are a good indicator that we are still on a journey because in case I haven't mentioned it, parenting is so freaking hard (I know I already mentioned it but some of you needed to know you are not alone in this ... again). And I don't enjoy it when my husband tells me that he loves my passion but that it can come across as disrespect to him, or that it doesn't help our kids when I act like a diva if I don't get my way. It actually sucks. But this is real life and vital to growth (don't worry—if you follow us on social—you also know he dotes on me all the time, outwardly proclaiming his devotion and adoration for me ... I can honestly say that we are more in love than we ever have been).

"The one who doesn't tell you what you want to hear, but tells you what you need to hear. Keep that." – Unknown

But I am grateful for a husband that communicates and doesn't just go silent. I am grateful that we are in this together. I have never had a person in my life fight for me and alongside me as I work to tame the beasts within like my husband does. He reminds me of what I am capable of and that I shouldn't settle for less. I could not be more grateful for the man I get to spend every day with and the way that he has contended for his health, his purpose and for our family. This book wouldn't be happening if it weren't for his support.

I tell you all of that not just to clear the air and totally lower your expectations of me, but also because I imagine many of you feel the same way. You know you better than anyone else does. You know your most authentic self, and you know when you are just playing a part. It's Jekyll and Hyde, right? You know the best and most beautiful parts of you, your greatest potential, and yet you are also well acquainted with the traits or patterns that, God forbid, everyone find out about. Here's the thing ... God hasn't disqualified you, but you have. Or unfortunately maybe someone else in your life has, in which I may want to call bluff on that person, seeing as I haven't really met a perfect person yet. If you are like me, you can list a thousand reasons why God should use someone else or why other people should have their dreams come true. The biggest problem when we operate with that mentality is that we are making it all about us. I heard someone recently say nerves are such a selfish emotion (Well, okay then). But it's actually true. Being nervous is putting the sole focus on me, versus on what I can bring to others. Rather, we should be making it about their benefit.

That was the tension in which I found myself. I had grown to like my quieter life, and I had learned to be content in the smallness of these last couple years. I learned to not just be okay with the fact that I would go to church and my kids' school and wherever else, being completely unnoticed and not a big deal, but to actually love it. Not that I ever was a big deal either. But I had been in places, both in Florida and Illinois, where it was common to see people I knew wherever I went, needed to be available most of the time and I always felt the need to be "on."

After much reflection and growth, I realized that for years I had been boldly and confidently preaching "at" people. Yes, I genuinely was coming from a place of love and didn't really know any better, but these last few years, I had learned new ways of communicating with people, the art of asking questions, and how to truly listen. Dan and I joke about how we would be much better pastors these days than we were before, now having been through the experiences and the training we received in not just the business and personal development world, but in our company specifically. Year after year, it became more and more apparent that we had been divinely led to where we were, but why? Just for us to become better people? For us to have a wonderful life? To help people get healthy physically and financially?

I knew better. There was more.

At this point in life, it simply couldn't be "all about me." I knew that God was asking me to step out and make a difference, not just for the temporary, but for the eternal. Ever have those moments where you want to be like, "Really, God?" And you sense His response is a little something like, "What? Now you *don't* want me to answer your prayers?" Coming off the bench wasn't just an act of obedience; it was an honor, and I knew it. I also knew it would require more work, more juggling and a whole ton of God-reliance.

I wanted to say yes to the obvious assignment I had been given, but how without going backwards? I had learned how to abide, how to slow down, and how to settle into this new lifestyle. Pursuing this might make me take up those old habits of striving and proving, and I was done with that.

I had to take a serious inventory of what was most important, what that original blank canvas dream was, and how I could finally get there now that God had given me the release. Could I chase my kids and my dreams and do it right this time? There was only one way to find out.

"Hope is not blind optimism. It's not ignoring the enormity of the task ahead or the roadblocks that stand in our path. It's not sitting on the sidelines or shirking from a fight. Hope is that thing inside us that insists, despite all evidence to the contrary that something better awaits us if we have to courage to reach for it, and work for it, and fight for it. Hope is the belief that destiny will not be written for us, but by us, by the men and women who are not content to settle for the world as it is, who have the courage to remake the world as it should be." – Barack Obama

Here is where I want to give you not just the "next section of my story," but share the practical things that I actually did. I have come to find these things are vital when wanting to pursue a dream, accomplish a goal, and get where you want to go. These steps are what I use on a daily basis, whether I am coaching someone in their health and in their business or if I am coaching myself from ground zero to launching what I believe will be a global movement of brave women pursuing their best selves and living their one and only lives in ways that make a difference and matter to them.

I am not going to go in depth with each of them, but trust me when I say, these aren't hard to understand; they are just difficult to implement on a day-to-day basis when the chaos of life ensues. But if you want that dream to happen, goal to be reached, or to live the life you desire, then I dare you to implement these game-changing actions.

1. Get Clear On What You Want

Seems simple, right? And yet I am often amazed at how many people are unhappy with where they are, but when asked to share clearly what it is that they desire, they can't even put words to their hopes and dreams. You can't get to a place when you don't know where you want to go. Try putting that address on the map. Good luck!

Start by getting crystal clear on what you want. Literally take yourself there a year from now, five years from now. Describe that place for me. What do your relationships look like? Describe your dream house, that school you want your kids to go to, that trip you want to take. Visualize it happening. In this desired life, what are you doing with your time, talents, and resources? How does that make you feel?

Now make sure to travel back to reality and write down in detail what you want. Make a vision board with pictures that keep you excited about what's possible. Look at those things daily. Then get real with where you are and what it's going to take to get there to that life of your dreams.

2. Make A Decision

Now that you know what you want, you just have to make the decision if you are going to commit to going for it. This could be the day and the week that changes everything ... I mean, why not?

It won't be because the stars all align and the doors of opportunity suddenly swing open.

It won't happen because you are now officially ready and no longer feel afraid. Or because everyone in your life will understand you and approve of you.

This will be the week that changes everything because YOU DECIDE it's going to be.

Because you quit getting paralyzed in thoughts and actually start doing.

Because you step out, take a risk, and obey the voice in your heart.

Because you choose to believe in yourself, in your dream, and to stop looking for permission and validation from others.

Because you only get one life, and waiting until tomorrow or next week just isn't going to cut it any longer.

3. Just Start

Do something TODAY that your future self will thank you for.

Break down your big dream into smaller goals. Get on paper what you need to do to get it done. Then ask yourself what you can do TODAY to just move in the direction of what you desire to accomplish. Then DO IT. No, really do it. Don't go to bed until that sucker is done.

It won't be perfect. You won't feel ready. But you just might realize that it's in the process of saying yes, stepping out and going for it that the victory happens one step at a time. The win isn't accomplishing the ultimate goal; the win is in putting in action today. Winning today will empower you and give you momentum to head into tomorrow and do it again.

Quit waiting for the right circumstances, the right emotions or the right YOU to start. The growth required in order for you to have the life you dream of happens in the midst of you pursuing it. So get after it! Today.

The first thing I did after my pink Bible moment and making the decision to go for it was not to try to figure out every little detail from start to finish or to get paralyzed in over-thinking. It was to ***JUST START***. So I made one phone call. Step one for me was reaching out to **ASK FOR HELP** and **ACCOUNTABILITY** because remember I work better with others than I do alone. I felt such a strong conviction that it was time to move forward in creating this community of world changing women, but I had a husband and three kids I was unwilling to sacrifice, no matter how great the cause.

Because of that, I picked up the phone and I called a good friend who had her own social media business, and I asked her to help me get started. One of the first goals I had was to start speaking into women's lives on social media and bringing value to them consistently. I already knew there was a huge audience who was hungry and ready for that, and I know this is hard to believe, but I had lots to say. I just needed someone with more expertise in that field. She had a designer's eye, believed in me and this mission, and would faithfully check in on me when the doubt would creep in. I knew she would speak truth to me when I would start to go rogue.

She patiently helped me create a logo, identify and clarify my brand and purpose, build a website for my blogs, and launch on social media platforms. I say patiently because I wasn't going to rush it this time. It took me awhile to find my rhythm.

4. Build A Support System

I think you get this by now, right? Are your people propelling you forward or holding you back? It's *essential* to have people in your life who believe in you and in your dream, a circle who is cheering you on. If you don't have that, create it. Start putting yourself in rooms and amongst others who are also chasing their dreams and bettering themselves.

You also need support as far as actual help goes—like finding a mother's day out program to drop your kiddos off so you can have some quality dream-building time. Maybe a high school girl to come over and watch the kids or help with the laundry and dishes a couple hours or a couple of times a week. Switch off with another mom ... take each other's kids once a week so you each can do what you want or need to get things done. It takes a village. If you refuse to ask for help or get support, you just won't make it very far. You'll be able to dream, to wish, but you will struggle to put feet to those dreams. It might also be good to ask yourself why you are unwilling to do so. Because it hurts your pride? Because you want everyone to think you can do it all? Because it costs too much? If any of these apply, you may need to ask what this dream is really worth to you.

5. Rearrange Your Priorities

"Whenever you say yes to something, there is less of you for something else. Make sure your yes is worth the less." – Louie Giglio

I had to learn that whenever I make a decision to commit to something new, I am simultaneously making a decision to quit something else. I can't just keep adding and adding, or I will soon burn out, or someone or something I love will pay the price. If I were going to do this right this time, I would need to change some things up.

One example: I had a goal to really get consistent with my weekly Brave Women Wednesday video calls. I loved interviewing, giving a voice to, and honoring key amazing women in my life that I knew would inspire our Team Brave Community. Remember—I wasn't in this for me! I was in it for them. I didn't need to be the solo act. I wanted it to be clear from the get go that this was a tribe of women who don't compete or compare; we celebrate one another. Yet currently I was on rotation to lead worship for the elementary chapel at my kids' school on Wednesday mornings. (Funny story ... I don't even sing, like, at all. But in an effort to help my middle girl get acclimated and bring some energy to their chapels, I started a kids' worship team. Pretty much we would lip sync and do motions to the songs. It was over the top cool. Oh, be quiet; you don't even know how awesome we were ☺.)

Anyway, when I made the decision to prioritize those video calls, I knew I needed to start showing up every Wednesday morning. So I let the administration know I was going to finish up that school year, but next year as my daughter moved to middle school, I also would be moving on to other things as well.

When pursuing a dream, your priorities and commitments need to be re-evaluated. How do you know if this is happening? Take a look at your calendar and your bank account. In essence, where are you spending your time and your money? This will reveal what you need to know. And if you aren't investing those things into making your dream a reality, then most likely you aren't really in PURSUIT.

In order to give yourself fully to the people and purposes you feel are a priority in this current season, you must guard your yes. Yes, you will probably let some people down. They won't get it. But they don't have to. You only get one life, remember? You want to be able to have no regrets about how you lived it. Protect your yes and save it for what and who matters most.

6. Lean Into Structure

I know I touched on this when I was becoming, but this is everything and where I see SO MANY women get stuck. When working with someone who has shared their dreams and goals with me but isn't moving forward, the problem almost always is that they don't want what they want bad enough to make the choices to do the work to get there. It's as simple as that. Might sound blunt or even rude, but often, the hard truths are. If you are going to chase dreams in the midst of a busy life or crazy circumstances, you will need structure. I often joke on our coach team trainings that I repeatedly have to tell myself again and again, "Structure is my friend ... structure is my friend."

I think if we were to be totally honest, many of us run our weeks based on situations, circumstances, and emotions. Or we put everyone else's stuff before our own.

It's vital to determine what the rocks in our schedule are as a couple, as individuals and as a family. Those go in to the calendar first. Then the pebbles, the sand, the water ... don't know the visual? Google it. For real, though. More room exists in your schedule than you think; you just need to get more strategic. Dan and I live by our calendar.

Plan the work; work the plan. I learned this back when we were working full-time, coaching in our "spare" time, and raising three young children. We had to lean into structure.

If you don't have a plan, you can't do the work.

It changed the game for us then, and I knew it would do that for me again when it came to this dream. Hoping and wishing are great, but they don't move you forward. Dare I even say, it isn't just when we throw prayers out to God that things often happen. It is when we make a decision to partner with our Creator to create. Things start to fall into place because they are *planned* to fall into place.

And I am not talking only calendar work stuff. You need to plan literally everything, including self-care activities. In the midst of pursuit, I have to prioritize taking care of myself. If I don't, then not only may I barely make it to the finish line, but I will be miserable and make everyone else miserable along the way. Don't be a martyr. Take care of yourself physically, mentally, emotionally, and spiritually so that you can enjoy the journey. Are there days when I am reading my Bible while I am brushing my teeth? Sure there are. But in reality, we find time or make time for what is important to us.

It can't ever be about what you FEEL that makes you act; it simply must be about your values. Draw the lines in the sand, create the structure, and make decisions based on those values and what you want most. Dan and I decided some non-negotiables a long time ago, and I needed to honor those even in THE PURSUIT of this new dream.

If we were going to keep building our business, and I was going to say yes to team brave and writing this book, we had to make sure our kids were taken care of. That meant extra help after school. That meant hard and fast rules, like not missing birthdays or big events. We'd pay extra or move the moon to make sure we would be present on all the important things. But if someone else shopped for our groceries? That is okay. We weren't missing the things that mattered to us or our children. Priorities.

If we were going to lean in to our kids doing after school and competitive activities and developing themselves, we would have to get even more creative to handle the time commitment. I made an intentional effort to meet and make friends with other cheer and dance moms, not only to make friends (yes!), but also to add to my village so that we could take turns and help each other out with rides, costumes, snacks, whatever.

The pursuit is a little bit messy, but that's okay. This season of teamwork and intentionality requires me to grow—in my capacity, in my compassion, in my passion for my business, marriage and my kids. Is it hard to find balance? I'm not even sure I believe there is such a thing. As my dear friend Jen Jones reminds me often—"It's not about balance. Life ebbs and flows. It's about finding your rhythm for this season." That makes way more sense to me than balance.

Does it take more planning and scheduling?

Yes.

Does it require more help?

You better believe it (doesn't have to be paid help. Think of family or other moms you can trade childcare days with—you get it. Be creative and get some help).

I am not willing to let our children suffer so that I can fulfill my dreams. It is Team Valentine. So I have determined to make sure that everyone is taken care of well as best as I can. I have traveled coast to coast to be there for Mariah's All Star Cheer competitions and Stasia's singing and dance performances. Literally. Last month, Mariah competed at Disney World in Orlando, and the next weekend, Stasia performed at Disneyland in Anaheim. Sometimes it's exhausting, but other times it is exhilarating. But I love having the front row seat to them chasing their dreams! And I have designed my life in a way where we all get to do that. Let me also balance that with the fact that I also don't feel the need to be room mom, or copy mom, or classroom party host mom anymore. There's mothers fighting over those positions, and I genuinely and graciously thank them for all they do. It's just not where I am at right now. You've got to find your place for this season.

7. Be Willing To Fail

I remember being a new mom and a first time youth pastor. One morning I stepped outside onto our front porch and called my mentor, Jeanne. I told her I didn't think I could do it all. It was harder than I thought it would be, and I felt like I was always failing. She asked me if I wanted to do both, and I told her absolutely yes. I will never forget what she said next. As only Jeanne could say (and those of you who know her recognize this), "My dearest Meg ... you are most assuredly going to fail. I would suggest you choose what you are going to fail at." Whew. I needed that permission to fail, but also the awakening that I get to decide what I am going to fail at.

Fail at laundry. An immaculate house. The gourmet dinners. Those were places I was willing to fail which of course, required a conversation with my husband. But I enlisted people to help. You see, anyone could do those things. But field trips with my kids. Date night with my husband. Being the one to put my kids to bed and pray with them at night. Those were the things I refused to fail at.

What are you willing to fail at so that you can have the time and energy to pursue that dream deep within your heart? What are the things most dear to you that must be guarded and protected?

8. Seek Mentorship

As you can tell, I believe in mentorship. This is a vital part of the pursuit. Actively pursue mentorship. This could be a coach, counselor, pastor, a leader in your field—in person or simply someone online. Do you know that some of my greatest mentors have no idea who I am? They are authors, Instagram inspirations, people on podcasts, singers, etc ... but also it's vital to have people that speak in to your life.

Those who speak to all the good things, but also people that are willing to speak the hard things. People you have not only given permission to coach you, but pretty much paid, begged, or at least requested to tell you what they see. We all have blind spots or misses that we need help identifying. Who in your life is willing to help you become the best you, even if their words sting?

Be coachable. What mindsets, habits, or relationships are a part of your life but are no longer serving you well? How badly do you want this new reality? Enough to hear the hard things, take them to heart, spit out the bones, take the gold and make the changes? Get yourself a coach and listen to what they say! (Side-note: a good coach spends more time asking questions than they do giving advice ... because let's be honest, often we know what we do and even know what is keeping us from doing it; we just need to uncover why and where to go from here).

After realizing that this venture would be different from others I had taken, I hired a life coach to help me get clear on what I did and did not want and what it would take to get me there. He helped me identify the obstacles getting in my way and actions I could take to overcome them. He connected me to other people that would cause me to grow, simply by being around them. He assisted me to really identify the crossroads, the two paths I could take, and who and what would be affected based upon my decision. The result of that help is one of the reasons that I still am here pushing through and writing this book.

Don't go at it alone.

9. Level Up

> *"It's your responsibility to manifest the greatness that is within you."*
>
> – Unknown

No more excuses, no more playing the blame game. This is your life, and it's time to take personal ownership. This is on you. In the midst of the pursuit, personal growth can't fall to the wayside. Does it take a lot to find time to read books, listen to podcasts, read the Bible, or to journal? To further your education in a subject that is imperative to reaching your goals? To network with people? Yes. Yes it does. But how about you trade in your Netflix, stay up a little later, get up a little earlier, turn off the radio, and make better use of the time you have been wasting. It is in the process of the pursuit of becoming our best selves and going for our dreams that we actually become the people who are ready to handle the dream within our hearts. It's why there is no short-cut. We wouldn't be ready or trustworthy otherwise. But in the process, in the battle, as we fight for these dreams, we grow in strength, mental fortitude, skills, character, and can then be prepared when that dream deep within our hearts becomes a reality.

10. Stay Consistent And Don't Give Up

It just has to be said. And we will talk more of this in the next chapter, so I am not going to get into it much, here. But hear me when I say, it is going to get hard. Even harder than you think. You are going to grow weary. You will deal with doubt, fear, criticism, and much more.

Keep showing up anyway. Keep going. Keep praying. Keep believing. Keep doing the work. Keep looking back at that vision board and what you want so you don't lose sight of why you started all of this. Keep on keepin' on, girl!

The awakening that I have had in the pursuit is that maybe, just maybe, I really could chase my dream *and* chase my kids and do it right. I mean, that was all I ever really wanted, anyway.

CHAPTER EIGHT

Resistance

"Most of us have two lives ... the life that we live and the unlived life within us that we dream of. Between the two stands Resistance"

– STEPHEN PRESSFIELD,
THE WAR OF ART (IT'S AMAZING! CHECK IT OUT!)

We have come this far. We have given ourselves permission to lean in to the stirring, to identify what it is that we really want and have taken the time to design a path to get there. We have people supporting us, and we have made a decision to go for it. To chase these dreams and goals, this God-given purpose within us that we are meant to fulfill, and then what meets us around the bend?

Resistance.

Any time you have a desired level of growth, resistance is going to occur. It just is. The larger the impact, the greater the resistance. If you are dreaming big and making serious plans, know that resistance is around the corner. If people are going to be impacted and if you are truly going to become the best version of yourself, trust me, resistance is on the way.

I have come to find that resistance exists both externally and internally. One of the first and most common forms of external resistance is LIFE. You really are set up to chase your dreams, do big things, map out your whole week, and line up everything in your calendar. You may make a conscious decision to live out of structure and not emotion. You may work hard to prioritize pursuing your best self, to make time for personal development and for connecting with key, life-giving people ... AND THEN ... you wake up sick, your kid gets sick, your babysitter cancels, you realize your calendar is filled with crazy amounts of last-minute school and sports stuff. Ugh. So now what?!

Listen. Life is going to happen. You will not always see it coming. Something will come and attempt to thwart your calendar, and in doing so, steal the time, energy, and focus you had prepared to put towards those dream-building activities.

Simply put, that is resistance.

So what can your response be?

Are you going to get frustrated, throw your hands up, and say forget it? Maybe next week will work out better? Or do you find new time? Create new white space? Say no to some other good things in order to say yes to the great things? Get up a little earlier and stay up a little later? I always say if that block in your schedule needs to move, no worries, but where is it getting moved to? Deleting isn't an option if you want to accomplish your goals and move forward.

Life will provide lots of opportunities that you could use as your excuse. I work with moms all the time that commit to building a better life for their kids, or work to be able to be more present with them, yet they then get frustrated because they aren't moving forward, and because they aren't taking the needed actions to get there. When I ask them why they say, "my kids." That's resistance. It just is, over and over. Don't allow your why to become your excuse. Remember what's on the other side of this crazy, messy season.

The chaos, the unexpected, and the unwanted things that happen in life will try to distract you from your purpose. Don't let them. Setbacks will come, discouragement will creep in, and disappointment will try to keep you down, but press on! Persevere. Your purpose is too important to let life get in the way.

YOUR PURPOSE IS TOO IMPORTANT TO LET LIFE GET IN THE WAY.

You see, once you've clarified what it is that you want or feel called to do, it becomes easier to design the path to get there. The dilemma is that when we set out on our path to achieve our personal success, we often feel like we aren't moving quickly enough. Things aren't as smooth as we would like them to be, the doubts and frustration begin to set in, and we start looking to the left and to the right.

Why aren't doors opening for me, but they are opening for her? As you are working hard, praying hard, and believing, you might look around and be tempted to feel like it's happening for everyone but you.

You are going to want to compare and compete.

That's resistance, and it's a trap that will slow you down and hold you back.

Don't give in.

Dare I Say It? Anxiety Is Real

I feel very strongly that I am supposed to pour some hope into some of you in this chapter regarding a few specific types of resistance that I dealt with personally (like anxiety, chronic pain, and critics) once I decided to really pursue some big dreams. Mainly because as I have been open about them in other arenas, so many of you have come forward saying you deal with them, too. As Christian women or women in general, I think much of the time we are not sure what our response should be when dealing with anxiety. What are our options? What is acceptable?

Please let me state before I dive into this topic that I am not a medical professional. I'm not giving you medical advice or a prescription because I don't know you or your specific situation. We are all different. I am just sharing my personal journey and some things that have helped me, and that I hope will help you.

Sometimes when we are in the thick of things, we get to that point where we accept that our situation is "just the way that it is." It's almost like we diagnose ourselves into a dark place.

Sometimes we receive some of those thoughts as fact, as truth, when actually, it is our job as children of God and women of the Word to fight for who we are and who God says we are. To recognize that our purpose is on the line.

About 18 months ago, in my pursuit of my best life, my anxiety went from sometimes-I'm-stressed and feeling-a-little-nervous to a paralyzing just-need-to-get-through-the-day anxiety. How do you chase your dreams and live your best life when you feel like you are just trying to survive?

Let me share a personal journal entry from December 16, 2017, to give you an idea of how I was feeling:

HOW DO YOU CHASE YOUR DREAMS AND LIVE YOUR BEST LIFE WHEN YOU FEEL LIKE YOU ARE JUST TRYING TO SURVIVE?

"I awake with such heaviness ... I don't want to get out of bed or face all the thoughts I am thinking and feelings I am feeling in the moment I first open my eyes. But the thoughts keep shooting at rapid momentum, and I can physically feel my heart rate increase—lying here is no longer an escape. It starts to feel like a trap. So I get up.

The anxiety begins to rise from within with so much to do, things I forgot, things I am afraid to forget. I hate it. I am awake for ten minutes and am already totally stressed out but, of course, don't want anyone to know because they absolutely deserve better. So I try to choose joy. But inevitably something happens or is said that triggers a stressed response, which elicits a negative interaction between me and one of the kids, or between Dan and me.

How desperately I long to break this cycle. I want genuine and authentic peace and joy. Will I always have to fight so hard against the negativity? The anxiety? Lord, please help me get to the bottom of it.

It feels silly and immature writing these things, but keeping them in is wreaking havoc on my body, my mind, and my life, so I am not doing that anymore."

Can you relate at all?

Listen. I do not for one minute believe that this is the thriving life that God has in mind for us. It is no way to enjoy an abundant life.

I had to work through all of these emotions. I had to realize that there is a level of, "I've got some stuff to deal with," but also there were choices I could make to move forward versus just giving in. I was in the process of taking care of my physical ailments, like my dental work and my back/hip pain, so why wouldn't I also work to move forward with this particular ailment? I remember realizing that my daily back pain was a detriment to all other areas of my life and thinking, "I don't want to live this way." Why wouldn't I approach my mental health just as aggressively?

Let me just take a moment to give a side note here that I think is really important: even now, a slight bit of a stigma still exists regarding mental health obstacles like depression and anxiety. I think sometimes it can be a pride issue when people view these struggles simply as a form of weakness instead of something that requires assistance. Or a fear issue because you have been told as a woman of faith that you are victorious, you just need to pray more and believe more. "What side of the cross are you living on?" They tell you God has already done the work, you just aren't receiving it. Or how about the people that dare to say any hidden doubt or sin does not bring healing, so that must be your issue? (Pardon me as I vomit.) These statements infuriate me to no end.

I have close friends who have battled sickness, lost children to cancer, dealt hardcore with postpartum issues, mourned a failed marriage, or struggled with depression. Can I tell you ... it was not because they lacked faith in what God was able to do or had hidden sin.

It's true that many of us struggle with feeling overwhelmed or feel down or not good enough from time to time. If this is something you are dealing with on a daily or consistent basis, please seek help. Help is out there, and it is for your good.

Hear me loud and clear: if you're feeling this way, you are not doing something wrong, but you can do something to move forward. You are not weak because you feel overwhelmed. You do not have to hide this struggle from everyone around you. Please hear me: you have permission to talk about it and to do what you can to fix it. To live a better life.

Find some people who can come alongside you; seek out a counselor; look for a physician who can speak into these issues and help you.

On the flip side, DON'T let what you're feeling become your excuse for everything. I've had days where I would tell Dan, "Honey, I just can't do that today because I'm feeling really overwhelmed.." or "Can you just take care of it? I don't have it in me today." Once in a while, that's fine, but over and over? That will wear on a marriage and a family. I began to label myself and just accept those feelings as a way of life. "Oh! I'm sorry. I can't do that because I deal with anxiety and pain."

Be careful. Yes, I may be feeling all of those things, but that does not have to dictate my behavior every day. I made a decision to keep pursuing my options to move forward, to see measurable results, and to find peace in my life. I refused to let this anxiety or pain become an excuse to avoid my life.

WHATEVER WE SPEAK OVER OURSELVES HAS SO MUCH POWER.

Whatever we speak over ourselves has so much power. Not only can what we speak come to pass, but it also can shape our beliefs. When we have those beliefs, we begin to base our actions out of them, keeping ourselves in a cycle. You can allow yourself to be honest with where you are, and yet still be intentional to speak what you want to see happen!

I'm not denying that I'm dealing with anxiety or pain. But I'm not going to speak all of the negativity over myself that will reinforce it or settle into the lie that it will always be this way.

One of the most common forms of internal resistance is found in our limiting beliefs or self-deprecating thoughts. These thoughts start showing up any time we want to grow, accept a challenge, or attempt something new or different—any time we are stretched beyond the familiar. There is power that comes when I identify what those thoughts and limiting beliefs are for me—the things that I have come to believe as truth when really, they are not.

The doubt, fear, insecurity, unmet expectations—they are all resistance.

- Am I good enough?
- Do I have what it takes?
- Does anyone even care what I have to say?
- Can I be a good mom and run a business/ministry?

All resistance.

Often we spend so much time questioning, over-thinking, and mulling over these concepts that we get paralyzed. We never move into action. If I choose to give in and believe those thoughts again and again, then they will imprison me. Ultimately, they will stop me from fulfilling my God-given purpose. When you and I commit to identify, call out, and work through these self-sabotaging thoughts, that's when the breakthrough really begins to take place. When we replace disbeliefs with truth, we will find a whole new freedom that energizes us to walk boldly and confidently in who we were created to be.

There are some areas in my life where I had simply just given up and sat down. Some areas of my life, I had just accepted as truth when God says differently. But I started to realize it was up to me if resistance would defeat me. It also confirmed that what

I was doing must matter and was worth fighting for. So instead of sitting down on the inside and the outside, it was time to make a decision to rise up and to take up my sword and my shield of faith and to engage in this battle.

God still heals! Miracles still happen! He still shows up in the middle of our situations. I don't have time to go into the countless stories in the Bible of healing that required action, but if doubt is a struggle for you, go check out the healing of the blind man, the woman with the issue of blood, the paralyzed man lowered through the roof, and all the others. These stories infuse me with faith and passion.

WHEN WE REPLACE DISBELIEFS WITH TRUTH, WE WILL FIND A WHOLE NEW FREEDOM THAT ENERGIZES US TO WALK BOLDLY AND CONFIDENTLY IN WHO WE WERE CREATED TO BE.

Yes. God is the miracle worker. But it is OUR job to seek, to knock, and to ask and believe. To stand on His word. To trust He is moving and to keep moving forward in faith and action.

Some of us have just taken a seat and thrown in the towel. "This is the way it's going to be." Or, "I've prayed, and it didn't happen."

We need to believe that God can still do miracles and can meet us right where we are. We need to re-open hope and our hearts to how capable God is.

I had to confess to God, and maybe you will, too, "I'm sorry I stopped believing, and stopped trusting that You can do this."

And then, don't be afraid to ask for help. Sure, from God. But also from other people. Evaluate if it would be helpful to see a doctor or counselor or just simply share your emotions with a trusted friend. Anxiety, depression, pain—all of these obstacles will tempt us to isolate which make things so much worse. We begin to believe that we must be the only person who feels this way. We believe that no one wants to hear our sob story and no one will really understand, anyway. Lies.

If anxiety or depression hits you in the face on a daily, or even weekly basis, if it is paralyzing you—no, really—you've got to do something about it. This is not the abundant life you have been promised. It is actually a lie. You owe it to yourself and your family to take care of it. Please remember the whole point of me even writing this book—you only get one chance to live your best life. If you're experiencing these afflictions, then you are not living your best life. More has been prepared for you. It pays off to get some help and to take care of them!

I hope you feel inspired that no matter what you are facing you can fight back. I have not overcome yet, but I am overcoming.

Paralyzing Pain Or Purposeful Pain?

One of the other largest battles and forms of resistance that I have faced is chronic—and sometimes even debilitating—pain. The past few years, I have had all kinds of physical issues ranging from needing my ovaries removed to oral surgeries that failed, to the biggest one for me—extreme and severe back pain that at times does not seem treatable.

Those of you who have experienced chronic, ongoing physical pain, you know that it's not just physical (I believe this applies to deep emotional pain as well). When that pain becomes so severe and so prominent, you can begin to lose the fight mentally, as well. Let me give you an example ...

It was early one morning, truthfully no different from any other day. As my eyes opened, I shifted to turn the alarm off, and pain immediately shot through my body. To be honest, in this season of my life, pain is an everyday thing. It is always there; it's just whether it's a level 3 pain or a 7 or a 9. It normally fluctuates throughout the day, but mornings are always rough. I would say that sometimes I don't want to get out of bed, and mentally, that's true. But physically, I HAVE to. My body cannot lie in that position any longer, and it normally takes a few hours for me to even loosen up. I have what looks like trauma to the spine, according to my MRI, that has created serious lower disc issues and pain that radiates throughout my back and down into my hips on a daily basis.

Here's the thing though: whether the pain is there or not, my kids need to get to school. Work needs to get done. People are expecting me places, life is happening, and I will show up. I just will. One of my best friends' mom has dealt with chronic pain for the last couple decades. I watched it steal her life. She lives on meds, barely ever leaves the house, and is no longer present or available for her husband or family. I think of this often and refuse to let this become me. I made a decision a long time ago to live my best life. I will do my very best to thrive, not just to survive. But I would be lying if I didn't admit there were days when I feel like that's exactly what I am doing: surviving.

It's hard sometimes.

Once I make it out of bed, I do the stretches that have been recommended from the multiple chiropractors and physical therapists and websites I have been to in the last four years.

Next, I rub a prescription cream from my naturopath on my back to help with inflammation, and then choose one of the eight over-the-counter gels or rubs or oils or patches that promises relief and use it like a Band-Aid.

I used to start my day with coffee, but now, instead of grabbing a mug off the counter, I reach for an ice pack from the freezer or heating pad, depending on the kind of pain I am having. I don't often feel hungry right away, but force myself to eat because I can't take any medication on an empty stomach. I pray that Advil or Tylenol will do the job and that I won't need to give in and take something stronger. Listen, though prescription meds do relieve my pain for hours, I hate the power they have. I hate how addiction to these pills has wrecked people's lives—people who matter to me, so I try to stay clear of them. Not to mention when I take them, I get all loopy and out of it and can't drive or write or do anything really productive. What a waste of my days that is! I can't live like that. No one should have to live like that.

But without them, I am in pain, standing at the bathroom counter trying to get ready for the day. I am in pain going up and down the stairs. I am in SO MUCH pain within just minutes of sitting in a plane, or my car, and especially driving (and since taxi driver is one of my main roles in this season of motherhood and I live in a city that is super spread out, I can't really avoid hours in the car on most days). By the time we get through school pickup, homework, dance or cheer drop off and pickup, working at the computer for hours, and all of the other things ... there are days when the tears start to fall while making dinner because I just can't ... I can't stand or sit or bear the pain and can't hold it in anymore. Those are the days I give in, I crawl up the stairs, and I dig out the stronger meds. I soak in an Epsom salt bath, put on more oils, gels, and patches, and fall into bed—sometimes before my kids get into theirs. My poor family (enter more guilt, exhaustion and frustration).

Honestly, there are days when I just feel absolutely done with it all. I hate pain! On my mentally weak days, I allow myself to put all the focus on pain management instead of on the active pursuit of health. If I am not careful, I can allow it to become an excuse. Even if it's a legitimate one, it's still an excuse. The pain drains me. I become tired, irritable, emotional, and easily frustrated, which results in me being unkind or short with my family, which is completely unacceptable.

Well, today ... it wasn't my family. Today it was the poor TSA agent at the airport. Insert red-faced angry emoji, then the anxious with one drop of sweat emoji, and then the cry face emoji.

We were catching a seven a.m. flight, so we were up by 3:45 a.m. in order to get to the airport on time. I had been extremely cautious to pack only the patches, gels, and meds that I could take in my carry-on and included one of those disposable ice packs that you just squeeze and pop and it turns ice cold. Please recall: back issues. I travel often, and with all the pain, I can get a bit anxious in the airport and just leading up to the trip. But I have found these ice packs to be a life-saver for long flights. FYI, they have made it through airport security all around the nation, even all the way to Africa and back ... EVERY. SINGLE. TIME. Until now.

So fast-forward. The agent is telling me I am pre-checked and don't need to take anything out of my bag, but I let her know I have the ice pack and that they normally want to see it and test it. She said, "mmmm ... okay," so I handed it to her.

"Nope. These aren't allowed."

"Ummmm, huh? I travel all the time and no one has ever given me trouble before. You can test it if you want, I just really need it for my back since this is a long flight."

"Nope. These aren't allowed."

Can you tell this was going south pretty quickly? It's early. I mean, I barely slept. I am already in excruciating pain. And now you want to take my ice pack away from me just because you can?! Are you freaking kidding me?! (All said in my mind only, thank God). I felt like a little girl who just got my comfort blankie ripped out of my arms. Wah wah wah. Okay, I know that's ridiculous—well now that I am looking back I do, anyway. In the moment, all I knew was that anxiety flooded in, but that's not what came out. The façade of pride and arrogance masked my feeling of exasperation. It wasn't about the ice; it was about the chronic pain I was sick of, and the fact that I felt like no one understood. This lady had no clue how much pain I was in, nor did she care to help. This is what I had been feeling in general (hello, victim mentality).

Pain can isolate. You don't want to throw a pity party cause no one wants to come to that type of party. I mean, come on! I don't even want to attend a party like that. You don't want to be the one always complaining and making excuses, or someone people don't want to be around. So you do your best to underplay it, try not to talk about it, even though it's hard not to because it's what you are dealing with every day. But you really feel like no one truly gets it anyway, so why bother?

I know ... Eeyore. And then there's the thought that I have every day. ... Sure, this really sucks, but I know so many more people going through things far worse than I am, so who am I to complain?

Back to the security line. Here's where I make you feel good about yourself as I describe how awful I was. By now, I am pretty sure my heart rate was escalating and my face was getting flushed, all sure signs I should have waved the white flag and walked away before doing something I would totally regret.

My response: "Okay, well do they sell these on the other side since you won't let me take it?" (Hint: I already knew they didn't).

"I don't know."

"All right. So for future reference, what am I allowed to bring through to take on the plane to ice my back?"

"You just can't have liquid. So you need to bring a frozen one."

"Ma'am, I am going to be traveling for the next eight hours. How am I supposed to keep a frozen one frozen?"

"I don't know."

"Okay. Well I guess you can have it then. Thanks so much for your help." Cue me stomping off.

Also cue completely embarrassed husband who was like, "Whoa! You need to chill a bit. We can get you ice somewhere else."

"I don't want to chill. This is stupid. I am just really frustrated right now."

Husband: "Obviously. And I don't want to be around you right now when you are like that."

Me: "Fine. I am going to get coffee. I will see you at the gate." I walked away and texted him almost immediately: "By the way, when you act like a big jerk, I have a lot more grace for you." To which he replied, "Well, you probably shouldn't." URGH!!!!!!!!!!

I walked into the airport bathroom, caught a glimpse of myself, and felt like dying as I read my sweatshirt that simply says, "Be kind." Once again, cue the tears. Overwhelmed with emotion, I was embarrassed of myself, I was angry that I had to deal with this pain (I was at least relieved that I was not wearing my "Jesus is Legit" shirt. It's one thing making myself look like an idiot but I hate making Him look bad). But I just looked at that girl in the mirror, and momentarily, my heart sank.

Here I am, the mom who tells her kids (and you) that nothing or no one gets to dictate your behavior except you. *You* control you. Here I am, the previous youth pastor, that told all those teenagers for all those years, don't follow your heart; lead it. Feelings are the F word. Here I am, the current health, life, and business coach, empowering my clients to stop, challenge and choose before responding.

"You can do hard things. You got this. Fight for the life you want. No one can sail or sink the ship except you."

Gag me. UGH. Do I believe those things?! Absolutely. Do I feel I have what it takes to live all that out today? Not so much. But I must. I must wipe my tears away, refuse to let my guilt overshadow God's grace, and start again. Not tomorrow, but right now. Life is too short. So I walked out of this bathroom, whispered for God to forgive me and to help me forgive myself. I took a deep breath, grabbed my coffee, and refused to let this pain or the negative emotions from earlier rule my day.

I arrived at the gate, sat down, and pulled up an article that a friend sent me the week before. The words in the article kept pulling me back ... I have looked at it multiple times and felt drawn back again that morning and sensed this part would be good to share:

"Your life is not happening in isolation. We tend to only focus on what is happening to us, not the impact our reaction may have on the lives of others. Maybe, just maybe, your suffering and pain isn't just about you. It could be you are impacting others for the kingdom, or that you are being prepared to be used by God to be a beautiful person, proclaiming the mysteries of God in a unique way from your life's experience. Something to ponder." – Unknown

And ponder I have. A lot.

I don't know why a lot of the things that have happened to me in life have happened. I don't know why two of my cousins committed suicide while we were in high school, one on my sixteenth birthday. I don't know why I had to go through painful relationships and break off an engagement to get what I have now. I don't know why key people that meant the world to me betrayed me and rocked my world and my ability to trust others for quite some time. I don't know why what should have been a normal surgical procedure with my teeth and jaw would turn into three failed surgeries over a span of two years filled with utter disappointment, pain, and frustration. I don't know why I have to be positive for the BRCA1 cancer gene and go through all the "hoopla" of mammograms and breast MRI's every six months and worry that what should be normal cysts might be cancerous. That at the age of 39, I need to be going through menopause and be put into a hormonal tailspin (again, sorry, husband and kids) because those ovaries just had to come out.

I also don't know why I have an amazing husband and perfectly imperfect marriage going on seventeen years when so many marriages around us have crumbled (we have, for real, fought for it, but you know what I mean). Or why I had three pregnancies and three healthy babies when people I love haven't. Why so many of my friends have lost a parent but I still get to have both of mine? Why do some people take a risk like we did with our career and changing everything in their lives and it didn't work out like it did with us?

It's all about perspective. Of course there are still times that I find myself asking God why, but that has become less and less the longer I have lived and the more I have come to know Him. God has never answered my "why" questions, and I will never understand why certain things happen or don't happen. What does He orchestrate versus what does He allow, and why?

We each have to resolve in our own hearts what to do with all of that. I personally choose to believe and stand by the promise in Jeremiah 29:11, that God's plans for me are good, and Romans 8:28, that "all things will work together for those that love God and live according to His purpose." I have no desire to have a theological debate with anyone about their beliefs, so don't bother emailing me about it unless you want to just be another number in that little red box in the corner of my mail icon on my homescreen (which trust me is high enough). Life is just too short. This is just a book about my journey, where I've been, where I've landed thus far, and all the in-between. And I can totally respect that that looks different for each of us.

What I have personally found helps me is changing my *why, God?* to *what, God?* Not why God is this happening? Or why do I have to deal with this? But what do you want me to do with this?

What I do know is that God has taken any pain that I have surrendered to him in the past and helped me find purpose through it all. God does not waste my pain. If I offer it up, He uses my story to encourage others. He wants to do that with your story and your life as well.

We all have stuff. We are all fighting battles. We all deal with pain. We all have something that we could use as an excuse.

This book has taken so much longer to write than I ever expected because I can't even sit for 30 minutes. If I take medication, I can't seem to gather my thoughts, and then there are the days (ummm, like right after being such an awful person to the TSA lady just doing her job) where I just flat out don't feel worthy of trying to help anyone else. But then I read that article again, and I see it, I hear it, I feel it ... and I just know it's true.

"MAYBE, JUST MAYBE, YOUR SUFFERING AND PAIN ISN'T JUST ABOUT YOU."

"Maybe, just maybe, your suffering and pain isn't just about you."

And so here I am ... sitting on the plane after a ridiculous morning typing this to you. Some things I have overcome. And some things I am still in the thick of.

And I imagine you are still in the thick of something, too. I am committing to you, and even more importantly committing to me, to continue to be relentless in my pursuit of my best self and my best life. And I would love for you to join me. We are all going to have days where we don't feel like it, or when we screw up and are the opposite person we set out to be that day. Join me from right there, in the thick of whatever yours is.

"The place your words come from matters: your words will come from the hurt of your heart or the hope of your soul." – Lysa Terkeurst

Resistance will try to make a victim out of you. But my friend, you are not a victim! You are an overcomer. If you choose to be intentional to lead yourself through whatever you are facing instead of succumbing to the anxiety, fear, comparison, emotional or physical pain you are dealing with, you will use all of that as fuel for your purpose. You will stop whining, making excuses, and you will start bringing hope to others as they watch you push through.

Speak hope to yourself and your situation (no need for ALL the details) and let others listen in ... you will be more likely to keep going and not give up, you will inspire yourself and others along the way, and you will begin to attract a tribe.

Don't wait to get through to the other side because just when you do, something else will most likely be waiting around the corner for you to deal with. There will never be a perfect time. You will most likely never feel ready. There's just stuff in life. Stuff we can't control. Situations, circumstances, emotions that will try to thwart our energy, our passion, our faith, too. That's why we need each other. We make each other brave. We help each other to not feel so alone. We remind each other that we CAN do this. We link arms, we and move forward together.

"Pain insists upon being attended to. God whispers to us in our pleasures, speaks in our consciences, but shouts in our pains." – C.S. Lewis

I don't know any other way to say this, but my reality is that: Pain demands a response. Real pain is right there looking you in the face. It won't go away. It distracts you, demands your attention, provokes you, and changes you. You get to a point where you can't simply avoid it, numb it out, or ignore it without consequences. It affects you and others close to you if it goes unaddressed. Pain tempts us to isolate. We feel alone, like no one understands, we are tempted to draw back and go inward. The way to fight that is to invest inwardly by drawing outwardly. Reaching out for help. Reaching out for relationship. Reaching out for resources to move forward.

Some of us are sitting around wallowing in pain, waiting for someone to notice. Waiting for someone to apologize. Some of us are paralyzed by hurt, anger, and fear and rightfully so. You may even truly be a victim, but you don't have to stay that way. In the same way, I don't sit at my house hoping that physical healing knocks on the door ... I am out there knocking on a lot of doors, trying it all, because I am in pursuit of healing and living this one and only life I have to its very fullest. I refuse to just accept this pain as my lot in life.

I get to choose.

And I choose to trust God and do what I can.

One of those doors I am knocking on daily is God's door. I am praying, hoping, and believing. James 4:8 tells us, "draw near to God and he will draw near to you." I step forward, and He meets me there. God has proven this true and been so faithful to show up in my life and pain always reminds me of this truth. And yes, in reality, there are days where I cry as I manage my disappointment when the spinal nerve block fails or when the epidural doesn't bring ANY relief, and I question if my most recent stem cell treatment is actually going to work. Some days I battle my doubt to trust the next doctor that looks at me and says he will help. But I choose again to stand on truth that God is a healer AND keep praying for wisdom as he directs my steps and my path. I wholeheartedly believe in the partnership of faith and works. I can pray for answers, but if I am not out pursuing them, I don't know that they would come.

So I have faith for healing. I trust. And I get out there looking for how God is going to bring it. I guard my heart and choose not to be bitter, but to call on Him. Is that easy? Nope. But have you ever hung out with someone that got hurt and didn't move past it? Someone bitter who has grown cynical and whose circle keeps getting smaller? Yeah, me, too. And that is not my future. I get to choose. So I may feel some of those things, but I release them and choose to fill my heart with hope and peace and love. And it's actually in these very vulnerable and lonely seasons that I find God close. The Bible says in Psalm 34:18, "The Lord is close to the brokenhearted and saves those who are crushed in spirit" (NIV).

I was catching up with a friend not that long ago who reached out to encourage me and let me know that my vulnerability was inspiring. She said to me something I pray I never forget. She said, "I hope you know your fight is not your own."

The reason that resonated with me is because it's true. It's what has kept me purpose-filled and passionate through years of pain and seasons of heartache and doubt. The thought that maybe, just maybe, I can take what I am going through, what I have overcome, and help someone else. What pushes me on the days I want to give in to all the doubt, fear, and insecurity that rises from within is ... well, it's you.

You think I can't see you. You think no one sees those dreams in your heart, those gifts and talents that are buried below the pain, the bills, the stress of everyday life. But you are seen. And you are known. And just like me, you get to choose. Courage is contagious, and so I will fight. I will break through and I will make space because I not only want to live my best life, but I want you to know there's a place for you to live yours. You get one life. And your purpose matters. You were created to impact others and leave a mark on this world. And if you haven't given yourself permission to live the abundant life that God has for you, one greater than anything you could ask for, seek or imagine, I pray that you would. It will be a fight ... but one worthy of the energy, passion, and sacrifice required.

IT'S SO HARD TO SEE PAIN AS A GIFT, BUT THAT'S BECAUSE WE ARE THINKING ABOUT A GIFT WE ARE RECEIVING AND NOT A GIFT WE ARE GIVING.

I look back on the many seasons of pain in my life, some physical and lots emotional. It is easier now to see the gift that came through that time. Finding the gift in the midst of the pain is difficult, but far from impossible. We simply must shift our perspective. It's so hard to see pain as a gift, but that's because we are thinking about a gift we are receiving and not a gift we are giving. Because this pain has humbled me, forced me to my knees ... as a woman with a lot of strength, perseverance, and grit, I find myself in complete dependence. Because of the things I have been through in the last forty years, I have compassion for people who have been through heartache, loss, physical pain. I have true empathy for people whose lives turned out differently than they expected. I have a listening ear, and a "you are not alone" mentality. I also have hope for them. I have Scriptures, a willingness to pray for them, believe with them, and words to remind them that life is short. There is so much you can't control, but do the best with what you've got. Count your blessings, share your story, bringing hope to others may be what heals you. Oh, wait! There *is* a gift for me in there after all.

Shake It Off

Thanks, Taylor Swift, for this timely reminder.

I can't end this chapter without mentioning a form of resistance that takes out so many during the pursuit. As you begin to live boldly, passionately, and confidently, you most likely will disrupt those who are around you. When an awakening or a big shift takes place in you, often what occurs is you rock other people's boats. As we have discussed, resistance is going to come in a number of different forms. If you are doing your thing right, it's definitely going to come in the form of critics and haters.

As you start living out loud and being bold about the new you, or about pursuing the life you want to live, these people will begin to step forward and get louder.

That's resistance.

You are making them uncomfortable because they are not pursuing *their* dreams. They themselves believe the doubts that you personally are not succumbing to.

Those critics are not getting out of their comfort zone and have no plans to. How can they be happy for you when most likely they aren't even happy for themselves? Does what they say really matter? If so, then you will waver, get quieter, and soon be paralyzed. Don't give them that power. This is your life. Is your purpose worth it? I believe it is, and I hope you do, too.

"You had a purpose before anyone had an opinion." – Rachel Hollis

Today, be reminded that you were created uniquely with love and intention to do amazing things and that being the best you is all you need to strive for.

Fix your gaze on your goal. Don't be distracted by looking to the right or to the left. (Go ahead and admire her, but don't change to be like her). Celebrate her, but don't compete with her. Be you ... boldly, beautifully, and confidently.

Pay no attention to the opinions of others who aren't putting themselves out there, taking risks, fighting for their dreams and contending to become the best versions of themselves (Keep in mind, people who are doing that usually honor that in others; they don't have the time or the negative energy to put into tearing others down).

Today, when things vie for your attention, energy, and emotion, ask yourself: Is this in line with fulfilling my personal purpose? If not, then consider moving in a direction that does. Make today count!

You are worth it. You were created to do big things. It is worth the push, the extra effort, and the time to become the best You and to fulfill your God-given destiny.

You may outgrow some people, and that is okay. Honestly, they aren't your greatest problem. Most likely, *you* are. You and you alone often have the potential to be your biggest obstacle, but remember the obstacle is the way. Which means: YOU ARE

THE WAY. Dig deep, stay consistent, and be committed to keep growing. Face into your issues as they arise in THE PURSUIT. Dig into the nitty gritty of your thoughts and habits that nobody else knows. Don't just go through resistance; grow through it.

We can look really good on the outside. We can show up and impress everyone around us. But if we don't internally figure out how to work through our need to please, our doubt, fear, insecurity, disappointment, or whatever else it may be, then we will not get where we feel God wants us to go.

Let me say it again. Our purposes are just too important to *not* work through our issues. I know I am called to awaken and inspire others to discover and pursue their best lives. That calling is too important for me to not work through my stuff. If I opt out of the process, then it won't only cost me, but it will cost all of the people God intended me to impact. And the same goes for you.

Resistance is going to come. Setbacks are on the way. May we choose to lean in and grow, to fight and press onward. What you are called to do is worth it. And so are the people that are on the other side of your obedience.

How we move through that resistance will absolutely determine the next phase of our lives.

Don't let anyone or anything hold you back. Keep on pushing until breakthrough comes!

CHAPTER NINE

Breakthrough

"You're going into a season where you are going to experience breakthrough after breakthrough because what you went through didn't break you."

– LISA BEVERE

I can recall a memory from about five years ago ... the big day had arrived. It was time to check "Great America" off the Valentine family summer bucket list. Everyone was excited! Everyone that is, except me. Don't get me wrong—I really wanted to spend time with my family and make great memories. It's just that over the past few years and as I have gotten older, anxiety and fear have become more of a real issue for me.

I have determined time and time again to not allow fear to set in or allow it to determine the direction of my choices. The feeling of fear can't be avoided, but that doesn't mean I need to give in to it. Right? I mean, aren't we supposed to say these things to ourselves? Because they are true and they are SUPPOSED to help.

And yet ... there we were. I could see the flags waving as we got closer, and my stomach began to drop. And we were only pulling into the parking lot! I felt my eyes widen as I stared at these giant, ever so high and winding roller coasters. My daughter began screaming, and I almost joined her, but for reasons different from hers. Not feeling that would be appropriate, I started some calm self-talk. "Megan, don't be ridiculous. Relax. Everything is going to be okay. Breathe. This is a day to have fun. You got this."

So we sunscreened up and headed in. My strategic husband and daughter had determined that we needed to ride the new Goliath roller coaster first to be sure that we got on it. Well—the wait was three hours. Pshhhhh ... yeah, right. After a quick pow-wow, we decided since someone had given us free tickets to get in that we should spend the money to buy fast passes, which would allow for a much greater and more memorable experience. Translation = we now have to—I mean get to—ride A LOT more roller coasters than I had originally expected. You see, waiting in line would have meant recovery time from the last ride and preparation for the new one, but not anymore. Oh boy ... time to do it.

Once we got the passes, we headed back to Goliath.

Goliath.

You know, David and Goliath? Goliath the giant?

Promoted as the TALLEST, STEEPEST, FASTEST wooden roller coaster that existed at the time. As I stood there looking up, I felt like I was going to pass out or puke, or maybe both at the same time. But onward we marched. We showed the park employee our fast passes and started walking and walking and walking. No stopping, no waiting. No time to prepare. Just up more and more stairs. Higher and higher we went. I felt light-headed and more than a little sweaty, and I began to realize that this would be very difficult to back down from at this point, even though that's what I most definitely wanted to do. I was ready to tell my family, "I'm out!" and run like a cowardly chicken back down those stairs. But I didn't. I just kept putting one foot in front of the other. And suddenly, we were there.

Our turn. There was no escaping, now. The thought began to run through my head, "I am going to die. No really, I am going to die." Yet I followed my nine-year-old, fearless daughter's lead and stepped onto the platform, sat down, and strapped in (as tightly as humanly possible I might add). I grabbed on to the measly little handle—seriously there wasn't even a bar in front to hold on to!! And like a flash, we took off. Up and down and all around ... we were flying through the sky—my family loved it!

Long story short, I not only survived, but I absolutely loved it, too!

The reason I wanted to share this with you is because after that ride as we were walking away, God connected the dots for me. It was like I could hear Him whisper that it's all up to me. I get to decide. You see I am on the ride of life and sometimes it takes me down roads I don't want to go. There are unexpected turns, dark places, and lots of unknown territory. There are also thrills, laughter, and a freedom that I would have never known if I opted out. Will I close my eyes, hang on for dear life, worry about everything that could go wrong and pray it goes by fast? Or will I strap myself in, throw my hands in the air and enjoy the adventure?

So for the rest of the day, I decided to say yes, take steps of faith, strap myself in and have a great time. We rode countless roller coasters and I felt like a kid again. It felt as though I was flying and free. Not to say that I didn't have to pray here and there and stop my mind from going to worrisome thoughts, because I did, but my mind did not get the best of me, and it created such a wonderful memory-making day.

The memory of this day and what God whispered in my heart continues to come back to my mind because it's so similar to my journey over the last four years. I may have not been facing Goliath the roller coaster, but I sure have faced many Goliaths, many giants along the way as I march onward towards the greatest adventure I have ever been on. And I had to do it ONE step at a time sometimes with heart racing and palms sweaty.

Your steps may be different from mine, but here is what I know: If you keep stepping and contending, breakthrough is coming.

You have read of my conscious steps as I faced my "Goliaths": prioritizing the Word and worship, leading myself through nutrition, exercise, and regulating of my hormones, asking for outside help, lots of sunshine, being fierce about my morning routine, leaning into structure versus emotion, building my team brave, a daily habit of gratitude, releasing expectations, and blooming where I was planted.

It was these steps and many more that led me to a place of breakthrough! A place I want you to all discover and experience for yourselves! How can I best describe this? The easiest description I can think of is "Maui."

Huh?

Allow me to explain. I don't know where your happy place is. Mine is Maui. It's the place where I come and just breathe easier, stress less, smile more, and slow down. I legitimately feel like I am living my best life and I am my best self here. I feel at home with myself here (I keep saying here because this chapter is actually being written from Maui). Do you have a place like that? I said to Dan, "I just like me more here." He said, "me too." HA! Not sure if that's a good thing or not.

We have always loved Maui but viewed it as a vacation spot, a paradise we could come to every once in awhile. About three years ago, we were invited to stay with some mentors and friends who had a house in Wailea, Maui. That week awakened us to new realms of possibility. They had a house there on the island, but also another up near family in Oregon. They would come to the island as much as they wanted and stay however long they wanted and the best part ... they let others use their house whenever they weren't using it. To see that kind of time and financial freedom, coupled with the abundance and generosity was a game-changer for us.

Dan and I began to visit Maui more and more. We would openly share and dream together of having a house here, of coming more often, and of figuring out how to adopt that same peace and joy wherever we are. We thought maybe down the road after the kids were gone, or in five to seven years, our dream of getting a place could become a reality. I started to believe it could happen. For fun, every once in awhile I would look on Zillow at places on the island and keep that dream alive.

A year and a half ago, I bought a hat on a girls' trip to Maui that simply said "808" and when people asked, I confidently let them know that it was my future area code. On another trip, I purchased a photo from a local boutique of one of my absolute favorite beach spots. I placed it in my office where I would see it everyday and it would remind me of that dream, of that happy place and that it would be worth it to do the work, sacrifice other things, and keep contending to see that dream come true. I kept telling myself one day that would be my view. In the spring of last year, we were hanging with friends in southern California, walking through some shops along the beach and came across a wind chime that I knew would be perfect for my future home in Hawaii (that didn't yet exist) and so I bought it.

I'll have to share with you the rest of the story later, but let me tell you that this past December we purchased our Maui home, fully furnished, years before I ever thought we would. Sight unseen, actually. Based on a friend's recommendation, we made a crazy offer that was contingent upon a walkthrough.

It was accepted!! What?!?! So Stasia and I flew here to make the final decision ... let me tell you, it didn't take long for me to know that this place was meant to be our place. What sealed the deal? I walked into the master bedroom, and wouldn't you know it, there hanging on the wall was the exact same picture that I had in my office of my favorite spot, only it was about 20 times the size of mine. This really would be my new view, just like I dreamed it would be!

Phew. Cue the tears. Not then, as I just had an overwhelming peace and a big smile while walking around with our new realtor and now friend, Kim. But tears now, as I sit here in my bed looking at this picture, and I work hard to finish this book.

I am beyond grateful and humbled for this life that I get to live on the other side of breakthrough. It was just over five years ago that Dan and I purchased a $200,000 home in Illinois that we needed my parents to co-sign on and assist us with the down payment. So yes, this took God, work, and breakthrough on many levels, including my view on and relationship with money. Don't get me wrong—I was so grateful when we didn't have to live paycheck to paycheck anymore (every once in a while, out of habit, I hold my breath when I put my card in the machine, and I keep an extra with me at all times, even though I know it's going to go through. But I have had to leave a few full grocery carts along the way, and that feeling sticks with you). Earning more money allowed for less stress and more choices, but when we started making incrementally more money than we ever had before, I definitely had mixed emotions ... gratitude, humility, guilt, doubt, until ... I realized all of the amazing things we could do with that money. We paid for kids to go to summer camp, partnered with more missionaries and ministries then ever before, and the best was being able to say yes and give whenever we felt led to do so!

"When good people make good money they do great things."
– Chris Harder

Dan and I felt a desire for this house, we spoke it, we believed for it, we worked hard for it and wouldn't you know, when Dan gave the green light to go for it, I panicked. *What?! This wasn't the plan; are you sure we are ready? Isn't it too soon,? What will people say? Life is crazy; how will we even get there*?

And his response ... "I want to do it now because I think of all the people who will use it when we can't. Our family, friends, the coaches on our team, the people who have impacted our lives and helped us become who we are. Let's get it for them." Yep. That's who I get to be married to. He has the biggest heart ever, and I am so glad he didn't let my emotions get in the way.

We call it our dream house not because it's our dream come true (though it is), but rather because we want others to come here and have dreams birthed in their hearts, awakenings of what is possible. We have loved every minute of every visit we have taken here, but in the six months that we have had this house, other people have used it far more than we have.

The first call my husband made when the house was finalized was to our kids' school to let them know they could use it as an auction item to raise funds. We have donated weeks to missionaries, pastors, and ministries that we love and support. I remember we were pastors and newly married when planning our first trip to Maui ... we took small increments out of each paycheck for two years in order to pay for it, so we get it! We love pastors and know how hard they work, how much they give, and how refreshing it would be for them to get away. It was our dream to bless them and so many others in our lives, and now we can. I am pretty sure our whole next calendar year for the house is already booked, and we love that! Before, I would probably not have shared all these things out of fear of judgment or fear that my motives would be questioned, but not after breakthrough. I so badly want you to see what is possible for you if you just keep putting one foot in front of the other. Not just a house in Maui, but whatever dreams and life you deeply desire. It's time to speak it, believe for it, and work for it to become a reality.

BREAKTHROUGH HAPPENS WHEN IT STOPS BEING ABOUT YOU.

What do I really want you to hear through all of this? Breakthrough happens when it stops being about you. Breakthrough took place when I stopped wasting time questioning my calling and recognized the truth that just because my assignment changed didn't mean my calling had. When I let go of titles and whatever image I was trying to keep up, in essence taking my eyes off of me, I recognized that I was not only doing the same work that I always had been, but I was doing it at a whole new level. Our success in the health, business and personal development worlds, our commitment to bring value whenever given the chance, and the trust we had built with people gave us voices into rooms that previously we never would have even been invited to sit in. The mentorship, training, and experiences provided to us over the last four years assisted us to develop skills that didn't keep us from our God-given talents, but rather enhanced them. The community and culture of our company fueled our passion for our mission, allowed us to partner with high level leaders, the biggest dreamers we know, and people that shared our belief that success = significance. And to remember—here I thought I was surrendering all my dreams and talents and this was going to be Dan's thing. Jeesh. Thank God for breakthrough.

Breakthrough happens when you open your eyes and stop putting God in a box. *Don't miss the answer to your prayers just because it looks different than you were expecting.* Here's the deal: when I prayed to be able to impact more people, get time and financial freedom so that we could give our talents and money away wherever we felt led, and to be able to provide a life that all three of our children would thrive in, I didn't realize it would mean leaving church ministry as we knew it. It would mean starting a new career, one many would question at first, that I would need to change and evolve so much ... but on the other side of breakthrough, I thank God every day for this life I am living. I know that I am not only exactly where I am supposed to be, but that I am just getting started.

DON'T MISS THE ANSWER TO YOUR PRAYERS JUST BECAUSE IT LOOKS DIFFERENT THAN YOU WERE EXPECTING.

Breakthrough happens when you can simultaneously live each day to its fullest *AND* yet are also intentional to do the actions today that will you move you closer to your desired future. Your efforts of working towards your personal goals don't have to and shouldn't cost your joy, ability to be present with those you love, or keep you in survival mode. *The best is here right now and is also yet to come.* Thank you, Thea, for reminding me that though there are great things to come, there are also amazing things right here where I am. I am going to miss out on them if I spend my time always wishing for what could be.

Breakthrough comes when we get in sync with what God is doing. ***Success comes when you partner faith with action.*** The life I desired was not going to come through simply throwing out prayers and having faith that it would just happen one day. Nor was it going to come because I was driven and self-reliant and determined to make it happen no matter the cost. It was going to become a reality because I partnered with the Creator to create. It is our partnership—like a dance—Him doing His part and me doing mine, that created a life of purpose, significance and fulfillment.

> *"And then the day came when the risk to remain tight in a bud was greater than the risk it took to bloom."*
>
> – Anais Nin

Do you really want to see breakthrough happen in your life?

I DON'T NEED ANYONE ELSE'S PERMISSION, INVITATION OR VALIDATION TO USE MY GIFTS.

I experienced complete and total freedom when I genuinely realized and accepted the truth that I don't need anyone else's permission, invitation or validation to use my gifts. In fact, 1 Timothy 4:14 tells us, "*Do not neglect the gift that is in you.*"

I kept waiting for people to notice what I thought I was good at, for opportunities to come my way. For doors to open on their own and without my doing. For invitations to start rolling in so I could use my gift and greatest passion. Once I had the breakthrough that God had uniquely created me, and in doing so, validated me—not based on anything that I had done but because I was His—I realized that His release was the only invitation that I needed.

With this newly found freedom and confidence, I began to dream and plan the Branded event—a one night "conference" for ladies—because I knew I had a message burning in my heart and it was time for it to get out. That event would not have happened without Jen and Thea, part of my Team Brave. We reserved a room for 400 women and I expected maybe 200 to show up. We ended up having to change locations to house the 700 women that registered for that night!

When I stepped out on that stage, I wasn't nervous ... I was *home*. Those ladies knew me. They were my people, my Brave Women Wednesday crew, my extended Team Brave. I didn't show up for me. I showed up because I felt so strongly that this message born out of my journey, pain, and breakthroughs was going to set many of them free.

You do you. So cliché, I know. You and I have probably heard it a million times, but breakthrough doesn't happen when you hear something, it happens when you believe something to the point that it loudly directs your daily choices. At nearly the age of 40, I finally gave myself permission no, that's not strong enough, I determined to make it a mandate to do me. My best me. I set out to discover myself, my likes and dislikes, my stress triggers, my joy producers, and the things that make me come alive. And just because it made the list before didn't mean it had to now. A clean slate for this season was what I needed for internal breakthrough. I started purging my closet, my home and my mind, saying good-bye to mindsets and habits that no longer served this new me.

In the process of finding me, I became passionate about wanting others to feel the freedom and joy of finding themselves, too. My message got clearer. I got bolder in life and online but was committed to stay authentic and vulnerable. I see so many women who are out there and have lots to say. They are hustling hard for those likes, comments, and followers. No judgment ... I have been there. Remember?

Let me share a secret with you, though. What I have found to be true in my life is that you can STRIVE to be an inspiration, DESIRE to be a mentor, or LONG to make a difference. You can WANT to be an influencer and put all this effort into TRYING HARD to lead people by imitating what you see others doing and what's working for them, by copying quotes off the internet or just creating a facade that that's what you are.

OR ...

You can just start PURSUING being the best version of yourself, LIVING that journey and that fight (cuz dang it's a fight) out loud (and I don't just mean the wins and the good parts), and INVITE other people to join you. You being you, you growing and getting better, you being authentic and relatable, you overcoming ... that's what will draw people to you. They will want to link arms, contend alongside of you, and celebrate wins with you.

If you are doing this thing right you will know because you will have people constantly telling you—not "I want to be just like you" but rather, "you make me want to best the best me."

Don't make the mistake of getting sucked into focusing only on followers, likes, comments and hashtags. Are these the metrics that determine true impact and success to you? (If so you can find lots of shortcuts). Breakthrough came for me when I was able to answer that question clearly and when I realized I cared less about those metrics and more about my growth. Have you figured out how to measure that? It's a game-changer when you do.

Strength really does come through the struggle. Brokenness is often the birthplace of breakthrough. When I quit fighting God and stopped wrestling with what was going on and why and instead chose to surrender and trust, well, that's when breakthrough could begin. When I chose to be honest with my current reality, embrace the obstacle as the way, and not just *go* through this season but *grow* through it, that's when amazing things started taking place.

"God made my life complete
when I placed all the pieces before him.
God rewrote the text of my life
when I opened the book of my heart to his eyes."

– Psalm 18:20,24 (MSG)

What if you recognized that all the crushing, breaking, and pain that you've experienced, all the good AND all the bad could be used for a great purpose? What if those same things you thought all along were weakening you were actually empowering you and preparing you for what is ahead? What if this is the path that leads you to what you have prayed for? Will you hang on long enough to get to the other side? And be patient enough in the process so that the full metamorphosis can take place? Don't stop now! What if your time is right around the corner?

Can you sense it yet? What breakthrough and freedom feels like? Can you envision finding home with yourself, right where you are, and being all in to creating what you desire most? If the roller coaster didn't do it, and Maui didn't do it, I have one last visual I want to give you ... *the spacious place.*

You see, as I travel back through the major breakthroughs in my life ... the decision to put God first, overcoming loss and regret, breaking off my first engagement, leaning into the stirring as Mariah turned ten, and taking that leap of faith into the unknown four years ago—they all had this in common. These events, emotions, seasons were causing me to feel confined in one way or another. They were defined by beliefs, relationships or commitments that limited me, and emotions that led me to feel trapped, out of control and anxious or restless. I knew there was more out there for me but the chaos of the everyday, the comfort of what I knew, the risk of failure, the approval of others—all of that imprisoned me.

I can remember exactly where I was the day I discovered the powerful, redemptive words in Psalm 18. I was in Rockford, Illinois, and it was spring of the year 2000. It was one of the first days that actually felt like spring; it was finally warm enough to throw a blanket on the front lawn, and so that's exactly what I did. I carried a book, my Bible, and a journal outside, thinking I would either read or nap. The air smelled of dirt and grass, and the sun shone warm and bright on my face. Honestly, I felt more alive than I had in quite a while.

It had been a long winter, not just physically, but emotionally and spiritually too. Breaking off my wedding engagement about three months prior had triggered a lot of doubt, fear, hurt, and confusion, which led me to a place of depression and isolation. And no one really seemed to understand. I was constantly around people, yet still felt so alone. I put on my "game face," but it masked so much pain and sadness. I showed up to pray, but after a while wasn't sure what to say anymore.

That warm day, I flipped open my Bible and landed in Psalm 18. These words jumped off the page to meet me right where I was at.

"He brought me out into a spacious place;
he rescued me because he delighted in me."

– Psalm 18:19 (NIV)

I believe it was not by accident that I happened upon these verses on that day. It was exactly what I needed! In such a real and personal way, in that moment, I could sense God's love for me, the way He was fighting for me. He wasn't satisfied to leave me in a dark and lonely place—He reached down, took me out, and drew me to Himself! HIS LOVE BROKE OPEN THE WAY. When I felt imprisoned and undeserving, He rescued me and brought me to "a spacious place." I was free! *If I allowed myself to be.* Why did He do this?!?! His word clearly says it is "because He delighted in me."

Talk about breakthrough.

Psalm 31:8 also talks of this place ...

"You have not handed me over to the enemy but have set my feet in a spacious place."

And so does Job 36:16:

"He is wooing you from the jaws of distress to a spacious place free from restriction."

I don't believe for even a moment that I should spend my one life confined, limited, restricted, or trapped. That does not equate to living my best life or being my best me. That's not the abundant life Jesus has offered me, nor one worthy of the ultimate sacrifice that he gave.

Galatians 5:1 (MSG) reminds us that "Christ has set us free to live a free life. So take your stand! Never again let anyone put a harness of slavery on you."

Breakthrough comes when:

- I recognize that I have become a slave to thoughts, mindsets and habits that confine me
- I take ownership and responsibility to change that
- I remove that harness and never let anyone put that back on me ... especially myself
- I accept the freedom offered to me
- I release the weight that has been holding me back
- I step into the spacious place God has set aside for me

I don't want to avoid things just because they're *hard* when greatness is on the other side. It's true. The struggle often gets the toughest right before the breakthrough, so if that's where you're at—hang on—you must be close! Some days I wanted to turn and run from my purpose, but here's the thing ... once you have climbed the staircase, locked arms with your tribe, said yes and meant it, visited the spacious place, it becomes too hard to turn back. You have come too far and too much is at stake. You will never be satisfied with anything less once you have tasted what is possible.

The passions and dreams in my heart are there for a reason. The pathway to get there may look different from what I had planned, but what I know is that when I keep the faith, trust the process and his promises, and do the work, that's when growth and *forward* motion will take place.

That's when the ultimate breakthrough happens. You go from stepping and stepping and stepping to strapping in and fully committing to the journey, and then you take off!! You can sense the momentum. You feel yourself cross over. Doors start to open. Self-confidence grows. The conscious choices aren't quite as hard because they are now habits that have created a new you. And you can be proud of that girl in the mirror because you have fought hard to become her. You finally feel at peace, at home with yourself.

So just know, beautiful but uncomfortable caterpillar: the agonizing part is almost over. You are so close to breaking free. The time is drawing near for you to spread your wings and fly!

CHAPTER TEN

One Life

"One life on this earth is all that we get,
whether that is enough or not enough,
and the obvious conclusion would seem
to be that at the very least we are fools
if we do not live it as fully and bravely
and as beautifully as we can."

– FREDERICK BUECHNER

I mean come on. Are you really surprised?! Of course, this is the last chapter, the final hurrah, the grand finale ...

ONE LIFE.

Oh, friend. I hope that by now, my passion has leapt from the pages of this book into the depths of your heart, but I wanted one last chance to speak life, hope, and truth to you as we wrap up this journey together. I wanted you to hear one more time that this life is yours for the taking! Don't wait a moment longer to lean in to the stirring and figure out what you want and then pursue it with all your heart. To become and unbecome and become again. To find your people. To fight the resistance and overcome. To have your breakthrough.

Because before you know it, you wake up one day, you look around, and you almost can't believe where you find yourself and how good it is.

Not because there are no obstacles, but because you no longer allow those obstacles to paralyze you. Not because people in your life are perfect, but because you have people. People who know you, believe in you, and won't let you settle.

Not because you have arrived, but because you are moving forward, accomplishing goals, and seeing dreams come true. You still battle your imperfections, but that's okay because you won't let them keep you from growing and stepping into the greatness you are capable of. You have a newfound freedom to say yes or no based on your purpose, your gifts, and what makes you come alive. You are at peace with the life you are building because it is centered around what matters most to you and what God has placed in your heart.

Your beliefs, values, and actions are more congruent than ever which makes you feel home right where you are. How do I know? Because I am there. Don't get me wrong. I still have my diva moments, yell at my family sometimes, and have to be intentional to not get sucked back in to striving and proving. But that's what they are—moments. That is not who I am.

I look around, and trust me when I say that there are plenty of days where I don't feel worthy to be entrusted with all God has given me. I mean, I have battled not feeling like I am enough since the age of fifteen. I can remember when the very seed of rejection and "not-enoughness" was planted in my heart as a freshman in high school.

Have you experienced the pain of rejection? The sting of comparison? Felt the need to prove you are good enough, smart enough, kind enough, pretty enough? Can you remember when the seed of "not enough" was planted in your heart? Can you recognize any beliefs or patterns that were formed because of that?

I can. And those lies surface from time to time. But you know what pulls me out of that place? That very self-centered space of making it about me and whether or not I am worthy? What pulls me out is the truth that I am enough. I am enough for Him. And you know what? I always have been ... even at my worst. It's hard for my mind to conceive, but the Bible tells me so. Romans 5:8 says, "But God demonstrated his great love for us by sending Christ to die for us while we were still sinners."

How can any of us hear this truth, truly receive it, and still doubt that we are enough? God did not wait until we had our act together, until we became our best selves, and we had proved our worth.

Instead, He gave us worth at our worst. How do you determine what something's value or worth really is? By how much someone is willing to pay for it, right?

We, at our worst, were worth God's very best.

WE, AT OUR WORST, WERE WORTH GOD'S VERY BEST.

1 Peter 1:18–19 says, "*For you know that God paid a ransom to save you from the empty life you inherited from your ancestors. And it was not paid with mere gold or silver, which lose their value. It was paid with the precious blood of Christ, the sinless, spotless Lamb of God.*"

I am not rejected.

I am chosen.

Accepted.

Loved.

I am enough, just as I am. Right here, right now. Forever and always. I may never be able to comprehend this, and maybe I will never feel worthy. But feelings don't dictate my life; truth does. And the truth is found right there in that verse.

God paid a ransom to save me from this EMPTY life ...

... and I refuse to waste this sacrifice—this ransom that was paid on my behalf with the precious blood of Christ.

In John 10:10, Jesus tells us that "the enemy came to steal, kill and destroy," and that's exactly what happens when I believe the lie that I am not worthy or enough. My joy is stolen, my relationships are destroyed, and I am distracted from my God-given purpose. My focus is on me instead of on God and all of that he created me to be and do. And I don't know about you, but the enemy has stolen enough from me. I am not giving him one more day.

Jesus goes on in that verse and tells us that he came to give life and life to the full. The Amplified version says (remember, this is Jesus is talking):

"I came so that they may have and enjoy life, and have it in abundance (to the full, til it overflowed").

Do you hear why Jesus came?! When he was in the garden, praying and asking God for another way—a way other than being hung on the cross when he didn't feel like going through with the plan, what made him do it anyway? Why? Why did he do it?

He did it for you and me.

He didn't just do it so we could exist and believe the lies and keep trying to be better and hopefully inspire someone along the way before our time is up and we die.

He did it so that we could have and ENJOY life: an abundant life—a life so full that it overflows on all the world around us in such a way that they want to know our God and live a life like ours—one full of truth, love, purpose and hope!

I hope you never settle for anything less than the abundant life that overflows. Receive the gift of Jesus and do not let it go to waste.

At our home in Arizona, we have a few citrus trees in our backyard. This was new for me after having lived in the Midwest for so long. I loved the smell of the flowers when they blossomed and couldn't wait for the fruit to grow! I envisioned sharing the lemons and oranges with our new neighbors and the teachers at school. I was busy traveling and living life, and one day I walked out into the backyard to do who knows what ... I actually don't remember because what is etched in my memory is the overwhelming sight of all the dying fruit, decaying under the beautiful trees, and the flies that would have a heyday.

I had missed my chance to pick so much of that fruit. I was busy doing other things. I was distracted. I wasn't paying attention. Those trees were not on my radar, and I had missed it. I looked at the fruit and I thought: what a waste! It made me sad.

And then I thought about this one and only life I had, and the two paths I had recently mapped out with my life coach.

One was a wide road, smooth and easy to travel, quite comfortable and safe, filled with friends, pleasure and quiet, and pretty much anything I could buy. The other was a narrow road, winding into the unknown, bumpy and uphill, overgrown in places, and it would require more of me if I was going to take the trek. There would be legs of the journey where the road could only fit one and I would have to march onward by myself. I would have to grow stronger, healthier, and be able to withstand more in order to make it. It was clear that it was the path with greater resistance; it was also the path of greater purpose, impact, and significance.

I knew God would love me no matter which path I chose. I knew that I could still live an abundant life and love deeply, regardless. But what drove my choice to the narrow road once more was all of those people coming behind me. I began to think about who would be affected if I took the easy path? What would happen if I opted out? If I didn't create and stay consistent with Team Brave? If I didn't finish the book? If I didn't go after all the other God dreams in my heart?

And I thought about what the fruit of my life would be versus could have been if I opted in to the "more" life?

I thought back to that rotting fruit. What a waste. A chance missed.

And it occurred to me that our lives are very similar. The days seem long, but we blink, and a decade has gone by. Your kids get older. Your dreams stay untouched. The day-to-day is still the day-to-day and nothing has changed.

One chance.

One Life.

The visual of that fruit has stuck with me as a reminder to not sit back or miss my moment. I have only one chance to get this life right! To live it fully! And to never let what I have go to waste.

Would it be easy? No, probably not. But it WOULD lead me to a life of joy, freedom, love, and a whole lot of fun.

On the other side of saying yes, you find yourself right there in the middle of creating and enjoying your best life ...

You're driving a hot pink Jeep down the backroads of the desert, chasing sunsets and singing at the top of your lungs to your favorite country hits and ...

Wait, hold up. What?

It's true. I totally drive a hot pink (pretty much the same exact color as the Mango Dragonfruit Refresher at Starbucks) Jeep Wrangler.

Without me knowing it, my husband had made arrangements to trade in his Jeep and purchased one for me that he had wrapped and specially designed according to a picture I had casually shown him a year before. I commented about how awesome it was and mentioned that it was my dream car. We joked about how most women my age or as their kids got older would dream of a BMW, an Audi, a Lexus, an Escalade, whatever, but not me. I wanted a hot pink Jeep. I didn't think about it much after that as I had a nice little Acadia that allowed me to do the job of mom-taxi just fine.

But on the morning of my 39th birthday, my husband walked me out to the driveway, and there she was in all her splendor! I couldn't believe it. I looked at him and at the Jeep and back at him, and then I just cried. I was so surprised and so grateful. That pink Jeep is like a physical representation of my free life. The time was right, and I was ready to rock that Jeep. Just a few years ago, I don't know that I would have been able to own something that was so bold, stands out a mile away, and draws so much attention. But my husband knows me and has been on the journey with me. He knew I was ready. And I can honestly tell you that for the first time, I really knew me, as well. I could step into what I call the "Pink Jeep Era," a season of confidence and freedom.

I get it. Pink Jeeps aren't for everyone, but you do you; I'm gonna do me. And love it.

> *"Our deepest fear is not that we are inadequate. Our deepest fear is that we are powerful beyond measure. It is our light, not our darkness that most frightens us. We ask ourselves, 'Who am I to be brilliant, gorgeous, talented, fabulous?' Actually, who are you not to be? You are a child of God. Your playing small does not serve the world. There is nothing enlightened about shrinking so that other people won't feel insecure around you. We are all meant to shine, as children do. We were born to manifest the glory of God that is within us. It's not just in some of us; it's in everyone. And as we let our own light shine, we unconsciously give other people permission to do the same. As we are liberated from our own fear, our presence automatically liberates others."*
>
> – Marianne Williamson

I was done playing small. Done shrinking. I was powerful and I knew it. Not because of me, but because of the light and the God within me. And I was ready to shine bright. And I had learned that in doing so, I would give others permission to do the same.

Sure, when you make a bold move, you get a response. And you figure out pretty quickly who your people are and who they aren't. The truth is that there are two kinds of people—the ones who think I'm crazy or too much, and the ones who LOVE it. There is no in between. No one on the fence. Either you're in, or you're out.

I will come back out to the parking lot after a Target or grocery run or whatever it was I had been doing, and it's not uncommon to have someone either standing by the Jeep, taking a picture of it, or want to talk to me about it.

Or—criticizing it.

One morning, I drove the Jeep to take the kids to school. The way the kids' school is set up, I dropped off the middle school girls first on one side and then drove around to the other side to drop off my elementary son, Micah. You know how the car line goes. I would inch along, pause, and wait while kids and some parents were walking through.

After a few minutes, what can only be described as an older, grumpy woman walked directly in front of us as we were stopped. It was very apparent that the Jeep caught her attention—and that she disapproved. She looked at me and the Jeep and literally shook her head and began to talk to herself. No one was around her; I can only assume she was informing herself of her opinion. It was as if I could see her lips form the word "ridiculous."

I literally laughed out loud. Luckily, the windows were rolled up, haha! I blew it off (former Megan would not have been able to do that). After I parked on the elementary side and walked Micah in, I started to head home.

The other schools where I live start a little bit later than our school, and so on the days that I don't stop to get coffee, I will pass by the neighborhood bus stop.

Well, on this day, I rounded the corner and saw all the kids laughing and playing around as they waited to be picked up. At the same time I noticed them, they noticed me.

One little girl who happened to be sporting a super glittery backpack, exactly the kind I would pick if I were seven-years-old, pivoted to see what everyone was looking at. The minute she turned and saw me, her eyes got wide, she leaned in and pointed right at me. With a burst of pure joy, she shrieked, "It's BARBIE!"

Oh, right. Barbie has a pink Jeep. Not an unflattering comparison if I'm honest.

I smiled and waved and played the Barbie part and tried to make her day. I mean after all, she had made mine.

I immediately realized—Grumpy Old Lady? You're not my people.

Glitter Backpack Girl? You are part of my tribe.

Life is too short to waste on the people who are never going to be your people.

"You cannot talk butterfly language with caterpillar people." – Timothy Leary

As I set out to pursue my best life and shine brightly, I discovered that not everyone would cheer me on. Critics started rising up, mainly from people with "computer courage," who most likely aren't out chasing their dreams because if they were, that's where their time and energy would go. Or maybe they tried and failed, and so now it's easier to criticize the ones who are still in the fight. Who knows? What I do know is that people I loved and trusted and I thought even knew me well opted not to support me, some through public posts, some in direct messages, and some to others behind my back.

I actually should thank those people because they only made me stronger. They helped me to recognize that I believe too much in my purpose to let anything or anyone stand in the way. And through questioning my motives and my actions and double-checking to make sure what they said was not true, I became more sure than ever before that I am honoring God the best way I know how, and that's what matters most.

You see, there is only one judgment that matters to me. It's that one spoken about in the Bible that will take place between me and My Maker when my life has reached its end. One day I will need to give account for how I spent my life … how I used the talents and resources that I was given. That is what keeps me going on the days I don't feel worthy or enough. That is what strengthens me on the days the critics take their low blows. I don't have time to waste judging others nor in worrying about others' judgments of me. I am too busy using my talents and resources in the best way I know how. I refuse to bury them or to play it safe.

You see, this ONE LIFE is the greatest gift that has ever been given to me. And I will not waste it on feelings of unworthiness, on what critics have to say, and on whatever else tries to hold me back or tie me down. I hope you won't, either.

"Once upon a time you were a little girl with big dreams that you promised you'd make real one day. Don't disappoint yourself." – Unknown

Through this journey, God has been resurrecting dreams in me from when I was that girl at the bus stop. You know, we lose that girl as we get older, in life and through all the "stuff" that we have to fight through. It's as if contending for your marriage and fighting for your kids—we don't take the time or have the energy to say, "what are the dreams within my heart?" And we lose that little girl in there who thinks that she can make a difference and can do anything in the world and is not afraid to go for her dreams.

I'm still that little Glitter Backpack Girl! I may be a grown up now and have a family and kids of my own, but I still want to travel the world, impact generations, and live my life to its fullest. The pink Jeep is what resurrects that for me.

I want to resurrect that for you. I want *you* to resurrect that for you. Climb inside my pink Jeep for a moment ...

I wish you could, literally. I would drive us through Starbucks and get coffee and take you on a drive to enjoy the beautiful scenery and skies of Arizona. And I would tell you ...

If you want to drive a pink Jeep, YOU CAN. If you want to create a circle of amazing friends around you, YOU CAN. If you want to write a book, YOU CAN. If you want to host a conference, YOU CAN. I don't know what it is for you. But YOU CAN.

YOU CAN and YOU SHOULD.

So ... what is your dream?

If you're not where you want to be, do something about it. Life is too short to show up every day to a job you don't like. If you don't love where you live, start looking elsewhere. If you are unhappy with your health, make a decision to change that, today.

You simply don't have to settle. Just because things have gone one way up until now doesn't mean that they have to stay that way. It only takes ONE person to change the trajectory of your life, and that person is you.

If you're worried about what it may mean to lunge ahead and forge that path to achieve your dreams that you are newly vocalizing, please be encouraged that your life does not have to be "either/or." It can absolutely be "both/and." The "and" Life. I am pretty passionate about this concept and grateful for my friend Jen Jones for sharing about it from the throes of her crazy and awesome life. I forged a way where I could chase my kids *and* chase my dreams—I don't have to choose between the two.

- I can do business AND do ministry.
- I can give my kids what they need AND prioritize my husband.
- I can be relentless AND know when to rest.
- I can have faith AND do the work.
- I can trust God AND do my part.
- I can have fun AND have fulfillment.
- I can be generous with my time, energy, talent AND take care of myself.

Too often, we think we have to choose. Well, in this year, this day, and this very moment (and moving forward), I am going to keep living the life of the "and" and let's be honest: you never know what else I may say yes to! It's my goal to inspire others to give it a try, too ... who knows? It may just be the path that leads you to the life you have been searching for.

Friends, the truth is, if one very flawed woman awakened to this realization of living a bigger life filled with joy, purpose, and authentic relationships had enough grit and faith to claim it as her own—so can you!

But if THOUSANDS of women did this and understood that they could raise their children to be anything they dreamed ... not by telling them ... but by showing them ... we could literally change the next generation! Part of that generation and my motivation includes my children Mariah, Stasia, Micah, my adopted-in-love daughter Allie, and all my nieces and nephews. I dedicated this book to them, and to you, and I meant it.

Well, here we are, my friends. As I wrap it up, hear me say: you are strong, beautiful, and powerful. May you never settle for less than your *best* life. On the days you grow weary, keep fighting, and remember that you are not alone and that God is for you. We are in this together. I pray you always feel the comfort and peace of being known by the One who created you. That you dare to risk allowing others to know the real you. And that you enjoy the journey of discovering the most authentic and best version of you possible. I truly believe you will also come to find that there's *No Place Like Known*.

About The Author

Megan Valentine is a wife, mama of three, and coach of all sorts. She is the founder of Team Brave: A community of women who are committed to pursuing their dreams, loving their people well, and living lives that matter. If she is not coasting down the Arizona highways blasting country tunes in her pink Jeep or oceanside with her man in the paradise of Maui, most likely you will find her in a "cheer mom" shirt at an all-star competition or in the front row, wide-eyed and beaming through one of her daughters' solos.

Instagram: @meganvalentine1

Website: www.mvalentine.com

Made in the USA
Las Vegas, NV
19 December 2020